LEANING ON
the
PROMISES
OF GOD
for
MOMS

SALLY CLARKSON

TYNDALE
MOMENTUM®

The Tyndale nonfiction imprint

Visit Tyndale online at tyndale.com.

Visit Tyndale Momentum online at tyndalemomentum.com.

TYNDALE, Tyndale's quill logo, *Tyndale Momentum*, and the Tyndale Momentum logo are registered trademarks of Tyndale House Ministries. Tyndale Momentum is the nonfiction imprint of Tyndale House Publishers, Carol Stream, Illinois.

Leaning on the Promises of God for Moms

Leaning on the Promises of God for Moms is adapted from *Mom Heart Moments* (Tyndale House Publishers, 2019), ISBN 978-1-4964-3210-0.

Designed by Dean H. Renninger and Libby Dykstra

Unless otherwise indicated, all Scripture quotations are taken from the *Holy Bible*, New Living Translation, copyright © 1996, 2004, 2015 by Tyndale House Foundation. Used by permission of Tyndale House Publishers, Carol Stream, Illinois 60188. All rights reserved.

Scripture quotations marked NIV are taken from the Holy Bible, New International Version,® NIV.® Copyright © 1973, 1978, 1984, 2011 by Biblica, Inc.® Used by permission. All rights reserved worldwide.

Scripture quotations marked NASB are taken from the New American Standard Bible,® copyright © 1960, 1962, 1963, 1968, 1971, 1972, 1973, 1975, 1977, 1995 by The Lockman Foundation. Used by permission.

Scripture quotations marked ESV are from the ESV® Bible (The Holy Bible, English Standard Version®), copyright © 2001 by Crossway, a publishing ministry of Good News Publishers. Used by permission. All rights reserved.

For information about special discounts for bulk purchases, please contact Tyndale House Publishers at csresponse@tyndale.com, or call 1-800-323-9400.

ISBN 978-1-4964-5095-1

Printed in the United States of America

27	26	25	24	23	22	21
7	6	5	4	3	2	1

A Note from the Author

Being a mother is profoundly important. Every day, your life is challenging, demanding, and on some days, you may even feel isolated as you fulfill this most important role. But you are not alone. God sees you and is with you. He created you to be a teacher, spiritual director, friend, and so much more to your children.

In fact, you, dear mother, are a hero. You are shaping the history of the next generation by choosing to be a lifegiving mother. You are a woman of great worth. You sacrifice your life daily to bring His life to your precious children, so that they can go into the world spiritually strong, emotionally healthy, and with a virtuous character intact.

This little promise book is my gift to you. It contains lifegiving messages and verses I hope will encourage you in your task, grant you wisdom, remind you that what you are doing will reap rewards for all eternity, and illuminate truths from His Word.

May He give wind to your sails and guide you through your journey with generous grace and His unfailing love.

Sally Clarkson

Lord, I pray that each woman who reads this book will be led by You. I pray You will provide them with insight, skill, love, wisdom, and the understanding of what it means to be filled with Your Spirit and to walk by faith in this journey of motherhood. And bless them with strength, joy, and a sense of affirmation in their great calling as parents. In the precious name of Jesus, amen.

MOTHERHOOD IS A MARATHON, NOT A SPRINT

I started out on the journey of motherhood assuming it would be a lovely adventure I would be able to accomplish with vibrancy and grace. I did not understand how truly long this walk would be, or about the blisters, hot sun, rough pavement, and curves I would face on the road ahead.

I hadn't counted on the weariness of being pregnant, giving birth, and nursing babies. I hadn't considered the ear infections, tantrums, messes and fusses, mounds of dirty dishes and clothes, and countless days to fill with meaningful occupation, not to mention the training, correcting, and instruction of my children in righteousness.

So many times, when I felt like I simply couldn't go on, I would creep away into my quiet corner to spend a few minutes with the Lord. Without fail, He would use those stolen moments to show me how important my role was in the spiritual life and heritage of my children. In those times, I glimpsed the goal of righteousness I was working toward and realized that I must reach it step by weary step.

I kept going by sheer faith and resolve because I could not ignore the ideals and calls of Scripture. With God's help, I chose to follow them and trust that they were blessed and right and would bring blessing to me and my family.

Motherhood is a marathon, not a sprint! Keep your eyes fixed on Jesus. Remember, you're in this for the long haul!

His Promises

Don't be afraid, for I am with you.
Don't be discouraged, for I am your God.
I will strengthen you and help you.
I will hold you up with my victorious right hand.
ISAIAH 41:10

God blesses those who patiently endure testing and temptation. Afterward they will receive the crown of life that God has promised to those who love him.
JAMES 1:12

He gives power to the weak
and strength to the powerless.
ISAIAH 40:29

IF MAMA
AIN'T HAPPY...

There's one thing children want that we seldom consider: a happy mama. Happiness is not always a feeling, but a choice that comes from a heart that desires to please God. Happiness is an attitude that says, "This is the day the Lord has made! I will rejoice and be glad in it." Of course, developing this attitude is another thing altogether. Here are some things I have done to cultivate happiness in my home:

- Greet your children or husband with a blessing when you first see them. Kiss your husband in front of your children—this makes them feel happy and secure. Take the time to tell him goodbye before he goes to work.
- Say things like, "I am the most blessed mama in the world to have you as my little boy." "Good morning, sunshine. I am happy to see you this morning!"

- Place things in your life that give you happiness or a sense of fun. Think flowers, walks at sunset, back rubs, sitting on the deck and watching the pines sway in the wind, etc.
- Practice being thankful every day—take time to look at the antics and into the eyes of your children and thank God that they are with you now.

Today, put some of these ideas into practice. And thank God when you see flowers, stars, color, sunsets, and all the other things He made for us to enjoy!

His Promises

Take delight in the LORD,
and he will give you your heart's desires.
PSALM 37:4

With joy you will drink deeply
from the fountain of salvation!
ISAIAH 12:3

You will show me the way of life,
granting me the joy of your presence
and the pleasures of living with you forever.
PSALM 16:11

LOOK FOR
THE SPARK!

Albert Einstein was one of the most brilliant think-
ers of his time. His name is synonymous with the
word *genius*. Yet, as a baby, his head was so large and
misshapen, his mother thought he was deformed. As
a child, he had a speech delay. He failed his college
entrance exam. Yet despite all this, he became one of
the most brilliant and world-changing scientists in
history.

Each child is qualified differently for performing
in life. How blessed is the child whose mother looks
for his or her unique design and personality, who
watches for the spark of interest her children show in
different subjects, who asks the Holy Spirit to show
her the place this child was crafted to invest his or her
life for God's glory.

God did not make any mistakes when He created
your children. Each child is fearfully and wonderfully
made. Consequently, we are wise when we accept them

as gifts from God and love, pray for, and validate them as He made them. We learn wisdom in life by leaning into His will and ways—and part of that is in accepting the children He gave us as they are.

Take the time today—and every day—to celebrate the differences in your children, to look for the genius, and to watch the life of God filling your home.

His Promises

God has given each of you a gift from his great variety of spiritual gifts. Use them well to serve one another.

1 PETER 4:10

Whatever is good and perfect is a gift coming down to us from God our Father, who created all the lights in the heavens. He never changes or casts a shifting shadow.

JAMES 1:17

In his grace, God has given us different gifts for doing certain things well.

ROMANS 12:6

SOUND INVESTMENTS

This labor of love that we mothers diligently pursue is not about now. It is about investing in the Kingdom of God. God has entrusted us with this charge of raising our children for His glory and we must complete our task with diligence.

Our hope is in Jesus. And because of Jesus, our labor is not in vain. If we connect to Him and listen to His words and admonition, we have reason for hope. We can have hope knowing that God sees us and has appointed us to steward the lives of little ones whose souls will have eternal impact.

We are investing in eternity. We are shaping history. We are giving shelter and nurturing, working to create a place where children can be taught wisdom, truth, and love in the stormy moments of life. Truth and purpose give us a reason to live this life of giving, serving, exhausting ourselves for the sake of living a story we won't see the result of for a long time.

We can live without this vision, experiencing our days as filled with endless, pointless work. Or we can live with it, and while our days will still be full of work, we can be assured that our work will have divine purpose.

His Promises

God is not unjust; he will not forget your work and the love you have shown him as you have helped his people and continue to help them. We want each of you to show this same diligence to the very end, so that what you hope for may be fully realized.

HEBREWS 6:10-11, NIV

"For I know the plans I have for you," says the LORD. "They are plans for good and not for disaster, to give you a future and a hope."

JEREMIAH 29:11

Now faith is the assurance of things hoped for, the conviction of things not seen.

HEBREWS 11:1, ESV

MENTOR, MOLDER, MOTHER

"The Mother is the fountain-head of the Home. The home is the fountain head of society and of the Church of Christ. And no influences in the universe contribute so much toward guiding immortal souls Heavenward as the Home and the Mother. If I were asked to name any one principle that seems to have an almost universal application, it would be this one: show me the mother and I will show you the man! Next to the sovereign grace of God, the influence of a mother's teachings and example is the most effective in moulding character and shaping destiny."[1]

These words, written over a hundred years ago, are still very powerful today. Often times, mothers replace conviction and vision with lots of activities and distractions for their children. As a result of all this rushing around to endless lessons and buying the newest

[1] Gene Fedele, ed., *Golden Thoughts of Mother, Home, and Heaven* (Gainesville, FL: Bridge-Logos, 2003), 221.

curriculum and technology for their children, moms feel like they are accomplishing something. However, a focus on home life is the key to civilizing our children and thereby our nation.

From the beginning of time, God created the home to be a place sufficient to nurture genius, excellence, graciousness, and grand civility. But the key factor is nothing that can be purchased or owned. The accomplishment of this grand life is found only in the soul of a mother personally mentoring her children through the power of the Holy Spirit.

His Promises

Direct your children onto the right path,
and when they are older, they will not leave it.

PROVERBS 22:6

And you must love the LORD your God with all your heart, all your soul, and all your strength. And you must commit yourselves wholeheartedly to these commands that I am giving you today. Repeat them again and again to your children. Talk about them when you are at home and when you are on the road, when you are going to bed and when you are getting up. Tie them to your hands and wear them on your forehead as reminders. Write them on the doorposts of your house and on your gates.

DEUTERONOMY 6:5-9

A house is built by wisdom
and becomes strong through good sense.
Through knowledge its rooms are filled
with all sorts of precious riches and valuables.

PROVERBS 24:3-4

INVISIBLE
STRINGS

It is in a personal relationship with a real person whose soul is alive that the deepest imprints of life are given. The secrets and deep emotions shared during the good-night hours, in which the soul of a child is tender and open; the comfort of warm, homemade food prepared and eaten in the early evening as ideas are discussed, prayers are said, and devotions are read; the advice given in the midst of washing dishes together after a meal; the heroic and riveting stories read aloud and enjoyed together that establish common patterns of morality, values, and dreams in the comfort of the blazing hearth; the mugs of steaming hot chocolate savored while squishing against each other on a couch—these are the heavenly moments when we can share God's Word with our children. His Word is food to the soul and nourishment to the mind and conscience of a child fully awake to all that is important in life.

There is no computer, television, software, or textbook that can pass on such passion, love, and motivation.

When the invisible strings of a mother's heart are tied to the hearts of her children through loving sacrifice and nurture, the stability and foundations of a nation become secure and stable.

A mother, living well in her God-ordained role, is of great beauty and inestimable value to the future of any generation. Her impact is irreplaceable and necessary to the spiritual formation of children who will be the adults of the next generation.

His Promises

You should clothe yourselves . . . with the beauty that comes from within, the unfading beauty of a gentle and quiet spirit, which is so precious to God.

1 PETER 3:4

If you prize wisdom, she will make you great.
*   Embrace her, and she will honor you.*
She will place a lovely wreath on your head;
*   she will present you with a beautiful crown.*

PROVERBS 4:8-9

When she speaks, her words are wise,
*   and she gives instructions with kindness.*

PROVERBS 31:26

WHATEVER
IT COSTS

We would never throw seeds out into the wind and expect them to grow into a beautiful garden. Similarly, we cannot throw our children out into the winds of culture and expect them to become people of great character and faith. This is especially true when media—the internet, television, movies, and magazines—and cultural values at large take commitment to marriage, purity, and godly character lightly. Both media and our culture scoff at those things and promote the adulation of celebrities such as actors, athletes, and musicians whose lifestyles are immoral and vain and who obviously reject those values.

When God places a child into our arms, we know it is one of the most significant treasures we will ever be given, because what we do to invest in that child's life will influence the course of history—not just that particular child's life but that of future generations.

Take the time and pay whatever it costs to be that

person in your children's lives, the one who gives them an appetite for God and the things of God. Make your home a place of real life, beauty, truth, and celebrated relationships, so that when you enter the gates of heaven, you can say to Jesus, "I did all that I could to whisper into the ears of my children the truths and secrets of the Kingdom of Heaven, and to pass on a love for You."

His Promises

Be an example to all believers in what you say, in the way you live, in your love, your faith, and your purity.

1 TIMOTHY 4:12

Imitate God, therefore, in everything you do, because you are his dear children.

EPHESIANS 5:1

Dear friend, don't let this bad example influence you. Follow only what is good. Remember that those who do good prove that they are God's children, and those who do evil prove that they do not know God.

3 JOHN 1:11

BEAUTY
TREATMENTS

We cannot pass on civility, beauty, intelligence, or excellence of mind and heart if we do not ourselves make these virtues a goal of our lives. As stewards of our souls, we must seek to cultivate a garden of beauty—it must be a regular habit, a discipline, to expose ourselves to great minds, the best musicians, fine artists, great theologians, and wonderful biographies, so that our souls will indeed reflect a museum of His great character and nobility—that of our great King.

There is so much ugliness in our world. The media is expert at creating new ways to celebrate and glorify evil, and it seems almost inescapable. Harsh realities are visually depicted for us on the news, in the papers, and online. If we don't intentionally pursue and reflect upon beauty, we will miss it as it is drowned out by the negative realities of life.

Creating an atmosphere of beauty, welcome, and hospitality takes work. I believe this is the work women in particular are called to do: to civilize, to make our domains beautiful, to invite others to see the life and glory of God.

Part of what God has done for us through Christ is to transform the way we experience all of life. He changes darkness to light and brings life to dead places!

His Promises

By his divine power, God has given us everything we need for living a godly life. We have received all of this by coming to know him, the one who called us to himself by means of his marvelous glory and excellence. And because of his glory and excellence, he has given us great and precious promises. These are the promises that enable you to share his divine nature and escape the world's corruption caused by human desires.

2 PETER 1:3-4

Yet God has made everything beautiful for its own time. He has planted eternity in the human heart, but even so, people cannot see the whole scope of God's work from beginning to end.

ECCLESIASTES 3:11

I pray that your love will overflow more and more, and that you will keep on growing in knowledge and understanding. For I want you to understand what really matters, so that you may live pure and blameless lives until the day of Christ's return.

PHILIPPIANS 1:9-10

DON'T GIVE UP!

Most everyone will give you permission to give up on your ideals. They'll say, "You deserve a break—you need to find fulfillment!" and so on. Yet we have just this one life to live a story that will show His excellence, His greatness, His love and mercy, His redemption and grace.

So many young women are listening to feminist voices, to popular culture, to contemporary thought. They do not know that certain choices, especially made after seeking the counsel of the wrong voices, will have great consequences in their lives. They unwittingly think that personal fulfillment comes from material things that will make them comfortable; work that will give them a sense of their own importance; experiences that will give them a surge of adventure and excitement; romance that will make them feel loved—but they do not really know or understand that in the long haul, no one and no thing can make them happy or fulfilled apart from the love and grace and forgiveness of God. So many decisions made for short-term gain have devastating consequences and leave ugly scars in the long run.

We must seek wisdom where it is to truly be found—within God's Word.

No one loves you or has more grace for you than God! He is a God of love, second chances, forgiveness. All He wants is our hearts. He wants to inform our decisions, our ways, our attitudes, our convictions, and our values, and He is waiting to talk to you . . . today!

His Promises

Tune your ears to wisdom
and concentrate on understanding. Cry out for insight
*   and ask for understanding.*
Search for them as you would for silver;
*   seek them like hidden treasures.*
Then you will understand what it means to fear the LORD,
*   and you will gain knowledge of God.*
For the LORD grants wisdom!
*   From his mouth come knowledge and understanding.*
He grants a treasure of common sense to the honest.
*   He is a shield to those who walk with integrity.*
He guards the paths of the just
*   and protects those who are faithful to him.*

PROVERBS 2:2-8

All Scripture is inspired by God and is useful to teach us what is true and to make us realize what is wrong in our lives. It corrects us when we are wrong and teaches us to do what is right.

2 TIMOTHY 3:16

Your word is a lamp to guide my feet
and a light for my path.

PSALM 119:105

TIME TO REFUEL

Being a mama is a long-term commitment. When you find yourself depleted, try to stop and take stock of what is going on in your life. Place your worries and anxieties in heaven. Simplify your schedule, plan a snack-style dinner of crackers and cheese or fruit and toast, and break out the paper plates. Planning other simple pleasures—making time for several cups of coffee or tea, having a nap, watching a show, or reading a magazine—helps too.

Refueling just a little, finding joy, creating pleasure, and celebrating life in the midst of all the demands, helps fill your heart up just enough to begin seeing light at the end of the tunnel. Slowly but surely, you will begin to see the miracles bubbling up. Our Father delights in providing for us when we take time to breathe, listen, and rest from the daily grind.

Take a day off from regular commitments and plan to be still. A woman with a Martha heart, frenetically busy, won't see the miracles of God, as she is so busy living in the whirlwind of her own making and subsisting in her own meek provisions that she loses all hope and becomes a wretched nag. Sitting at the feet of Jesus instead, and just having some respite, will do wonders to change the day.

His Promises

Don't copy the behavior and customs of this world, but let God transform you into a new person by changing the way you think. Then you will learn to know God's will for you, which is good and pleasing and perfect.

ROMANS 12:2

And this same God who takes care of me will supply all your needs from his glorious riches, which have been given to us in Jesus Christ.

PHILIPPIANS 4:19

Don't worry about anything; instead, pray about everything. Tell God what you need and thank Him for all he has done. Then you will experience God's peace, which exceeds anything we can understand. His peace will guard your hearts and minds as you live in Jesus Christ.

PHILIPPIANS 4:6-7

A MODEL PARENT

If you want to truly disciple your children, you have to model love yourself. You can't just say, "Jesus said we are supposed to love one another." If you want it to truly sink in, you have to do what Jesus did: spend focused time listening to the ones you love; give words of life and build them up; have fun, shared experiences with them; minister to them when they are sick or tired; appreciate their dreams; support and forgive them when they have failed. Then they do not just hear love as a word, but they experience love as a reality.

Similarly, if we want to change our own culture, we can't just tell people what is right and wrong; they must experience what is right by seeing it in our lives. We show people a realistic picture of marriage and family by inviting them into our home for meals, loving them actively and sharing Christ with them.

The role of motherhood is also extremely important in our days, just as it has always been! We must build our family culture in such a way that it builds anchor lines from our children's hearts to our hearts, giving them a reason to always think of home as the best place to be. Then, we must invite others into our home so they, too, will catch the idea of having a strong family culture and seek to build one for themselves. The best way to do both? Model Jesus so those around us can see Him.

His Promises

Be kind to one another, tenderhearted, forgiving one another, as God in Christ forgave you.

EPHESIANS 4:32, ESV

Since God chose you to be the holy people he loves, you must clothe yourselves with tenderhearted mercy, kindness, humility, gentleness, and patience.

COLOSSIANS 3:12

Therefore, whenever we have the opportunity, we should do good to everyone—especially to those in the family of faith.

GALATIANS 6:10

UNCONDITIONAL LOVE

If we are to please Christ, there is no other option—we are commanded to love. Unconditional, grace-giving love must be our commitment, standard, and model every day if we want our children to know the Lord and commit their lives to Him. None of us is perfectly mature or strong in these areas; I have felt disqualified in this role as a mom many times when I became angry or irritated or said unkind words. But the ideal I get back to is to ask for forgiveness, give grace, and verbalize love. As we strive toward and practice God's ideals, our children will be given a foundation of emotional security.

The reverse is also true. If we harbor bitterness toward others, if we are regularly critical of people and do not forgive those who have offended us, we are leaving our children a wrong image of God, for we are their picture of His love and lovingkindness. Our words might say, "Love one another," but our actions may not. While many areas factor into rebellion, some children rebel because of hypocrisy in their home, where critical, pharisaical attitudes were the norm, rather than love—and it produced children who did not know God because the reality of His love was not the predominant character quality they witnessed.

Living together at home offers multiple opportunities on a daily basis for us to practice forgiveness! Perhaps we need to be reminded so often of our own need for God's forgiveness.

His Promises

Love your enemies! Do good to them. Lend to them without expecting to be repaid. Then your reward from heaven will be very great, and you will truly be acting as children of the Most High, for he is kind to those who are unthankful and wicked.

LUKE 6:35

Love is patient and kind. Love is not jealous or boastful or proud or rude. It does not demand its own way. It is not irritable, and it keeps no record of being wronged. It does not rejoice about injustice but rejoices whenever the truth wins out. Love never gives up, never loses faith, is always hopeful, and endures through every circumstance.

1 CORINTHIANS 13:4-7

Don't just pretend to love others. Really love them. Hate what is wrong. Hold tightly to what is good. Love each other with genuine affection, and take delight in honoring each other.

ROMANS 12:9-10

BREAKING
THE CYCLE

Sometimes people believe that because their own pasts were difficult, it is impossible for them to create a life-giving home for their families. I have known many excellent women over the years who had extremely difficult backgrounds. By following the Lord through studying and obeying His Word, they became beautiful reflections of Christ. It's a question of priority: Who will you spend the most time with? Who will you pay the most attention to? Whose voice will you tune your ear to hear? Whose words will be held nearest to your heart?

How can you become a lifegiving person, whether you had a lifegiving background or not? Determine that you will read the Word of God every day. Choose to believe in and trust Him each moment, in every circumstance. Pray for His guidance and know that His presence goes with you. It is the engaged, loving heart that points others to Jesus, the wellspring of life.

There is nothing else to replace it—no cleverness or self-strength or rules or formula that can replace the palpable life that comes from living day by day, holding on to God's hand.

Do you want your children to draw from the life that is bubbling over from your heart, mind, words, and attitudes? Then you must spend day after day with the Word of Life who will give you the true source of wisdom and love you long for. Even as a house is built one brick at a time and yet has the potential of becoming a mansion, so a wise woman builds her house—one brick at a time—into a home of spirituality that comes from spending regular time with Him.

His Promises

For the word of God is alive and powerful. It is sharper than the sharpest two-edged sword, cutting between soul and spirit, between joint and marrow. It exposes our innermost thoughts and desires.

HEBREWS 4:12

Study this Book of Instruction continually. Meditate on it day and night so you will be sure to obey everything written in it. Only then will you prosper and succeed in all you do.

JOSHUA 1:8

If you abide in me, and my words abide in you, ask whatever you wish, and it will be done for you.

JOHN 15:7, ESV

TIME WELL SPENT

If mothers make their homes places of excellence, cultivate reverence for and worship of God as well as love for each other, spend personal time teaching and discipling their children, serve them through this training and nurture, and give up their own time to accomplish all of this, there will be hope.

When mothers abandon this important responsibility, there is a greater tendency for children to become the kind of adults who are self-centered and self-serving and who overlook unrighteousness without any pang of conscience, because that conscience has never been developed. For effective parenting to occur, there must be hundreds—thousands—of dinners made, laundry loads run, backs scratched, and cookies baked. There must be watercolor projects and messes, hikes and games of hide-and-seek, wonderful lifegiving books and concerts and the theater. Time spent ministering to our children is time well spent, because that investment grants us the door to their hearts. When their hearts are soft to us because we have ministered to their needs, their minds will also be softened to hear our values, our convictions, and our guidance.

Moms, the way you invest your life today will indeed have a great impact on history. The cultivating and raising of great souls is of the utmost importance. Your life is making a difference. Spend time in the Word, read those books that call you to excellence, pray with friends of like mind—and don't give up!

His Promises

And you yourself must be an example to them by doing good works of every kind. Let everything you do reflect the integrity and seriousness of your teaching.

TITUS 2:7

In the same way, let your good deeds shine out for all to see, so that everyone will praise your heavenly Father.

MATTHEW 5:16

For their command is a lamp
and their instruction a light;
their corrective discipline
is the way to life.

PROVERBS 6:23

PIT STOP

Life sometimes seems to be an obstacle course. How we face each dip that must be straddled, each curve that must be managed, each barrier that must be jumped will indeed determine the outcome of the race. There is rarely a reprieve, and we always have to be on the alert so that our souls stay in the place of peace and hope.

We want to always go to the place where the truth is, where God's presence is, giving us guidance and hope. Struggling through difficulties is normal, and we will still sometimes feel weariness, frustration, fear, and hopelessness right in the midst of feeling joy, deep appreciation, and love. But we must continue persistently looking for His treasures of encouragement and truth.

Make seeking God a daily priority. Set aside a time when no one will talk to you or disturb your reverie. Light candles, brew a cup of tea, and enter into the presence of the Lord. Sit for a few minutes and take in the peace of being quiet and still. If you struggle to calm your soul and instead stew and fret, try to gather your wits, spend time in His Word, and dig for new truth and knowledge. He is the one Friend to whom you can go every day. Without Him, there is no solution. Without His help and strength, there is no peace.

His Promises

But when you pray, go away by yourself, shut the door behind you, and pray to your Father in private. Then your Father, who sees everything, will reward you.

MATTHEW 6:6

Be still, and know that I am God!

PSALM 46:10

Seek the Kingdom of God above all else, and live righteously, and he will give you everything you need.

MATTHEW 6:33

THE POWER
OF WORDS

Words have deep and abiding power. They can give hope, redemption, and life; or they can bring guilt, anger, and death. We are to be stewards of our words, and if we are walking with God, we are to plant words as seeds in the hearts of our children, developing the fruit of life, beauty, hope, and confidence in them. I have talked to a number of moms lately who struggle with anger and impatience and find themselves yelling a lot at their children. Of course, all of us have experienced this—especially if we've been mamas for a while! We must remind ourselves that if we sow angry, condemning, guilt-producing words, we will produce children who feel hurt, condemned, guilty, criticized, and unloved. If we are to grow in righteousness, we need to use self-control in this area of angry words and learn to move more and more into His gracious, patient love as we mature.

Think of what would happen if our children

grew up on lifegiving words: "I am so thankful for you!" "You are a blessing to me." "I appreciate you because . . ." "God has a special place for you in His Kingdom." "You encourage me." "I see that you are capable in _____ area." "You are a joy." "You are faithful." "I believe in you." "I believe in your dreams." There would be stored up in their hearts a deep confidence that they are loved, respected, appreciated, and called by God to accomplish great things for His Kingdom.

His Promises

Don't use foul or abusive language. Let everything you say be good and helpful, so that your words will be an encouragement to those who hear them.

EPHESIANS 4:29

A gentle answer deflects anger,
but harsh words make tempers flare.

PROVERBS 15:1

Watch your tongue and keep your mouth shut,
and you will stay out of trouble.

PROVERBS 21:23

THIS IS US...

To be transformed means to become something other, to be changed into something different. And the idea of being transformed in order not to be conformed to the world applies so clearly to family culture.

The more we can do to instill a sense of "This is who we are," "This is why we believe," and "This is what we stand for," the better chance we and our children will have of resisting the urge to conform to the world. A family culture that is distinct and grace giving has the power to both change and protect us.

It won't happen by accident, however. Establishing and shaping a family culture requires intentionality, thoughtful planning, commitment, and sacrifice. But the result can be truly transformative.

We must construct a strong, definitive, faith-giving, biblical family culture. Then those in our homes will be better able to resist the compromising draw of the world because they will have been shaped and changed by the place where they spend the majority of their days. If they grow up steeped in Scripture and truth, beautiful and lifegiving practices, and the sacrificial example of love at home, chances are they will carry these virtues with them. In the absence of such foundational shaping, they will by default go the way of the world.

His Promises

Love each other. Just as I have loved you, you should love each other. Your love for one another will prove to the world that you are my disciples.

JOHN 13:34-35

As for me and my family, we will serve the LORD.

JOSHUA 24:15

You are the light of the world—like a city on a hilltop that cannot be hidden. No one lights a lamp and then puts it under a basket. Instead, a lamp is placed on a stand, where it gives light to everyone in the house. In the same way, let your good deeds shine out for all to see, so that everyone will praise your heavenly Father.

MATTHEW 5:14-16

FACE TIME

Conversation is becoming a lost art. Technology makes it so easy to communicate that we become accustomed to lazy forms of messaging. Instead of meeting a friend for tea, we send a text. Instead of dropping into an office to ask a question, we hide our request behind an email. Instead of working out a disagreement with a friend, we write an anonymous rant in a blog comment.

While digital communication, social media, and even snail mail are helpful in connecting us with others, especially those far away, they lack the personal, satisfying, impacting effect of a face-to-face conversation complete with questions, answers, smiles, laughter, tears, and even touch.

This is a great loss. One of the essential parts of being human is our capacity for connection. We are made in the image of a triune God, which is to say a relational God. To reflect His image is to live in communion with and response to our fellow image bearers. Texts and emails and even videoconferencing can bring us only so close to that kind of relationship. Sooner or later we need to have a direct connection.

If we are to live into God's fullness for us and be skilled disciplers, we must pursue the art of conversation. Through your example, teach your children to be "quick to listen, slow to speak, and slow to get angry" (James 1:19). Let your dinner table be the training grounds for graciousness and consideration.

His Promises

For where two or three gather together as my followers, I am there among them.
MATTHEW 18:20

Two people are better off than one, for they can help each other succeed. If one person falls, the other can reach out and help. But someone who falls alone is in real trouble. Likewise, two people lying close together can keep each other warm. But how can one be warm alone? A person standing alone can be attacked and defeated, but two can stand back-to-back and conquer. Three are even better, for a triple-braided cord is not easily broken.
ECCLESIASTES 4:9-12

*A friend is always loyal,
    and a brother is born to help in time of need.*
PROVERBS 17:17

24/7

Christians sometimes feel a pressure to be "spiritual" all the time. But to separate the spiritual from the ordinary is to say that Jesus is not King over those everyday moments in life. We should learn from Jesus to embrace the mundane moments—even the silly, fun ones—and find God's fingerprints of grace within them. If we can do this, we will learn to see God in a fuller dimension.

Jesus didn't come just to save our souls; He came to redeem every part of our lives. When we give our whole lives to Him—food, drink, work, play, body, spirit, and family—we glorify God by living into the beauty He meant for us.

I like to picture what the feasts in the Bible must have been like. In the time when Jesus lived, meals were not nice, orderly things. I imagine dusty garments, loud arguments, pungent spices, and stinky feet. Jesus' ministry not only allowed for these meals; it took place in the context of them.

Not all holy moments are somber and serious. If Jesus discipled His apostles in the midst of food, drink, laughter, and mundane moments, I believe we should too. Instead of viewing them as spiritual "downtime," we should see them as the times when God is most likely to work.

Our laughter can glorify God as much as our thoughtful meditation.

Serving pizza to a houseful of teenagers can strike spiritual gold.

We must learn to cherish all the moments of our lives and to call them holy.

His Promises

He will once again fill your mouth with laughter
and your lips with shouts of joy.
    JOB 8:21

So rejoice in the LORD and be glad, all you who obey him!
    Shout for joy, all you whose hearts are pure!
    PSALM 32:11

For everything there is a season, a time for every activity
        under heaven.
    A time to be born and a time to die. A time to plant
        and a time to harvest.
A time to kill and a time to heal. A time to tear down and
        a time to build up.

A time to cry and a time to laugh. A time to grieve and a time to dance.

A time to scatter stones and a time to gather stones. A time to embrace and a time to turn away.

A time to search and a time to quit searching. A time to keep and a time to throw away.

A time to tear and a time to mend. A time to be quiet and a time to speak.

A time to love and a time to hate. A time for war and a time for peace.

ECCLESIASTES 3:1-8

CAN WE TALK?

If we want our family and friends to feel they are a priority in our lives, we must regularly set aside time to invite them into our space.

There's a limit to what we can do to protect those we love from what the world throws at them. But we can listen and help them sort out their thoughts and feelings—if we choose to make ourselves available when they need us.

Making yourself available to friends and family is a choice you need to make again and again—the choice to forge a deep connection with them. Become the confidant for your children, so that as they grow older, they will know they can come to you at any time.

Jesus modeled this throughout the Gospels. Immediate availability was the way He operated. He answered questions when they were asked. He made a point of going off alone with His disciples to provide them with focused attention. And often He did this over food. In fact, He gave the most strategic talks of His life as His best friends and most devoted disciples were filling their stomachs with warm food (what could be better than fish over an open fire?), and they sat listening to His wisdom as their ease and comfort opened their hearts.

We would do well, I think, to follow His example.

His Promises

Don't look out only for your own interests, but take an interest in others, too.

PHILIPPIANS 2:4

Tune your ears to wisdom,
and concentrate on understanding.

PROVERBS 2:2

Sympathize with each other. Love each other as brothers and sisters. Be tenderhearted, and keep a humble attitude.

1 PETER 3:8

WALKING
THE WALK

How does a mother walk with integrity and righteousness?

We follow the example of God before us. In Genesis
1, we read that in the beginning, the world was form-
less, void, and dark. But God is the Creator. It is part of
His divine nature to create and bring forth something
new. So He, in His goodness, spoke light, beauty, color,
form, meaning, and love into the darkness and void.

What is our role, then? It is to follow His example.
With His grace in our hearts, we partner with Him.
We dispel our own darkness by choosing to walk in the
light. We bring the living, resurrection power of Christ
into the moments of our lives so that our children can
learn how the Christian life is lived by watching us.

In situations when we are unjustly hurt, we choose
to forgive and love unconditionally. In situations
where we feel abandoned, we choose to believe in
God's goodness and live in hope.

We practice telling the truth. We give back money

when someone has inadvertently overpaid us. We ask our children to forgive us when we have wronged them, teaching them humility through a relationship with us. We seek to bow our knee to God's will, even when it doesn't seem pleasant, so that they learn how to bow their will to God. We live with the Holy Spirit working visibly through us, producing love, joy, peace, patience, kindness, goodness, faithfulness, gentleness, and self-control.

His Promises

Look straight ahead,
and fix your eyes on what lies before you.
Mark out a straight path for your feet;
stay on the safe path.
Don't get sidetracked;
keep your feet from following evil.

PROVERBS 4:25-27

And now, dear brothers and sisters, one final thing. Fix your thoughts on what is true, and honorable, and right, and pure, and lovely, and admirable. Think about things that are excellent and worthy of praise.

PHILIPPIANS 4:8

The purpose of my instruction is that all believers would be filled with love that comes from a pure heart, a clear conscience, and genuine faith.

1 TIMOTHY 1:5

AT YOUR SERVICE

One of our greatest responsibilities is to walk through the days of our lives seeking to love our King and promote His Kingdom. One of the primary ways we do this is in teaching our children and modeling for them what it means to be a devoted servant of the King. We show them what it means to enter into the battle, to be willing to serve and give of ourselves. We are the ones who paint them a picture of the great battle, the great King, and their parts in fighting for redemption.

God has designed all of us with the purpose of being a part of His redemptive Kingdom work. Our children's hearts long to be a part of a great cause. Mothers can cultivate compassion for a lost world in the hearts of their children and show them how they can practically be a part of God's Kingdom work.

In the secular world, everyone's attention is turned on who is the most famous or powerful or has the biggest salary. By the world's standards, the call is not to service in the fight for redemption; it is to self-protection and self-fulfillment.

But from God's point of view, history is the account of human souls joining into the battle for the righteous Kingdom. Each of us is given a unique opportunity to live out a story in which we employ the moments, money, talents, and relationships of our lives to promote the priorities that are on the heart of the King, the Lord Jesus.

His Promises

And I have been a constant example of how you can help those in need by working hard. You should remember the words of the Lord Jesus: "It is more blessed to give than to receive."

ACTS 20:35

For even the Son of Man came not to be served but to serve others and to give his life as a ransom for many.

MATTHEW 20:28

For you have been called to live in freedom, my brothers and sisters. But don't use your freedom to satisfy your sinful nature. Instead, use your freedom to serve one another in love.

GALATIANS 5:13

THE PRESENT
OF PRESENCE

Our lives as mothers are often filled up with hurry and demand: chores, lists, and a multitude of responsibilities. There are so many ideals we feel we absolutely must live up to: clean houses, ordered lives, and children who accurately know math and Scripture and play their instruments perfectly, besides having just the right number of friends and activities. In the face of so much urgent need, our "Martha" lives often take over as we contemplate how to get it all done.

Yet these demands and ideals, the constant busyness and bustle, are not what will actually reach the hearts of our children and shape them into beautiful souls.

Christ did not create disciples who would literally die out of their love for Him by giving them a list of moral rules or commandments on how to live. What He gave them was the gift of His own very present life. He lived with them so that they experienced His love intimately throughout the moments of their days. He showed them what it meant to be a servant leader by healing, comforting, and compassionately sharing His loving redemption with needy and humble people.

Jesus showed us mothers how to disciple our children by being a model Himself. He laid down His life, not just in death, but also day by day with the souls He was shaping. This is what mothers do as well, laying down our lives for our children in order to create disciples for Christ with deep, rich souls.

His Promises

The generous will prosper;
   those who refresh others will themselves be refreshed.
   PROVERBS 11:25

Share each other's burdens, and in this way obey the law of Christ.
   GALATIANS 6:2

Dear children, let's not merely say that we love each other; let us show the truth by our actions.
   1 JOHN 3:18

ONE DAY
AT A TIME

To follow Jesus, we must carry our cross. We must give up our lives, die to ourselves—our expectations, dreams, and rights—in order to be surrendered to His Kingdom and His work. This, of course, goes against the world's priorities and is not understood by most people. We must be single-minded, as all good soldiers must be in a war, and remain faithful to Christ.

We are not of this world but rather waiting for the time when we will spend eternity with Jesus in heaven. We must prepare our children for this and model to them the type of sacrifice it requires from Jesus' followers to lose their lives for His sake. Serving in love is the bottom line, even if it costs us our lives.

Moms, God is calling us to a work that is quite important—He will give us the strength and supply us with wisdom one day at a time. He will listen to our prayers. But most of all, we have to be willing to bend over backwards to meet our children's needs, to encourage them, to help them figure out a new game plan when necessary, because we are God's guards in a fallen, tempting world. We are His hands, His words of comfort and wisdom, His voice to tell our children that we love them and believe in them because God loves and believes in them, even in the midst of their immaturity.

His Promises

Whoever wants to be first must take last place and be the servant of everyone else.

MARK 9:35

For this is how God loved the world: He gave his one and only Son, so that everyone who believes in him will not perish but have eternal life.

JOHN 3:16

I once thought these things were valuable, but now I consider them worthless because of what Christ has done. Yes, everything else is worthless when compared with the infinite value of knowing Christ Jesus my Lord. For his sake I have discarded everything else, counting it all as garbage, so that I could gain Christ

PHILIPPIANS 3:7-8

BETTER
TOGETHER

I remember watching the sunrise with one of my best friends when I was a young teen. We bundled up and took flasks of coffee to keep us warm in the early morning chill. Picking a soft spot of grass, we watched in awe as the sun rose in all its golden glory. Something about it caused us to think about true and beautiful things, and we ended up sharing our dreams of what life might be.

While the sunrise would have been just as lovely had I watched it on my own, it would not have been as meaningful. Having someone to share the moment with sealed the experience as a moment of significance in my life.

I believe this is how true friendships impact our lives. In friendship we share beauty, acknowledge significant moments, and cherish memories that sustain us through life. We become companionable witnesses to God's goodness, witnesses who can later remind one another who we are and to whom we belong.

We are so much more vulnerable to attack when we are alone. It is easier to become depressed, defeated, or prideful without friends who cheer us, correct us, and fight for our good. When we reach points of deep discouragement, convinced we can never progress, true friends lift our heads and say, "Remember who you are! God has worked, and He will again."

His Promises

Love each other with genuine affection, and take delight in honoring each other.

ROMANS 12:10

As iron sharpens iron,
*   so a friend sharpens a friend.*

PROVERBS 27:17

There is no greater love than to lay down one's life for one's friends.

JOHN 15:13

GROWING
PAINS

There is a mysterious point when a child no longer wants to be "mommy-ed" but will turn away toward the process of becoming an adult. No amount of seeking to retrieve the innocent years will make this new phase go away. Suddenly, it is God's time for your children to begin growing up! Until that time, there is a window of opportunity to pour in foundations of morality, truth, values, habits, and character, but then, suddenly, your whole relationship with your children will hit a roadblock, and you know that there will be a detour ahead—a different route to go!

So if you find yourself in the stages of new hormones and feelings expressed through your children, now, for a moment, ask yourself the question, "When I am having a bout with hormones and anger or rage or emotions come upon me with no warning, how do I want others to behave toward me?"

When we're grouchy, we want people to treat us

gently and to give us grace, understanding that this is not our usual behavior! And so our children want this from us, that we would take seriously Jesus' admonition to "do to others as you would have them do to you" (Luke 6:31, NIV).

During this phase, it is important to gently hold their hearts in respect, rather than treating them as small children and focusing on their failures.

His Promises

I am leaving you with a gift—peace of mind and heart. And the peace I give is a gift the world cannot give. So don't be troubled or afraid.

JOHN 14:27

I have told you all this so that you may have peace in me. Here on earth you will have many trials and sorrows. But take heart, because I have overcome the world.

JOHN 16:33

Make allowance for each other's faults, and forgive anyone who offends you. Remember, the Lord forgave you, so you must forgive others.

COLOSSIANS 3:13

YOUR STORY

Once a man and woman commit to getting married, they begin writing a brand-new story that has never been told before. It will be their heritage—the way they love each other, the way they live before God, the children they bring into the world, the homes they build, the impact they have on history, the stand they take for God and His Kingdom. The wedding day is potentially the beginning of a great epic. The tale that is written, of course, will not just be about the two— there are children, aunts, uncles, cousins, and more, both present and future, who will be affected by the quality and soundness and vision of a marriage and the choices the husband and wife make.

We have to choose not to give our children a legacy of compromise, disloyalty, and brokenness, and that choice will not be without cost. The way a husband and wife treat each other has a direct effect on how a child builds his or her internal sense of being.

And the stability of the home affects a child's physical, emotional, intellectual, and spiritual health to an infinite degree.

While many promote a do-what-makes-you-happy ethic these days, the truth of God's Word is timeless. He intended marriage to be for life, and we honor Him when we honor the covenant we've made.

His Promises

Always be humble and gentle. Be patient with each other, making allowance for each other's faults because of your love. Make every effort to keep yourselves united in the Spirit, binding yourselves together with peace.

EPHESIANS 4:2-3

Dear friends, let us continue to love one another, for love comes from God. Anyone who loves is a child of God and knows God.

1 JOHN 4:7

So again I say, each man must love his wife as he loves himself, and the wife must respect her husband.

EPHESIANS 5:33

WAITING ROOM

It seems to be a hallmark of mature Christians to have a story of having to wait years and years on God and then seeing Him come through with beauty, wisdom, and grace. But the Bible is full of people who took matters into their own hands when they thought God needed a little help, and it created all sorts of havoc.

When Abraham got tired of waiting, he got his maidservant pregnant and caused all sorts of problems (Genesis 16:1-16; 21:8-21).

Saul was terrified by the approaching Philistine army, and instead of waiting on God for how to proceed, he consulted a medium—something God had explicitly warned against (1 Samuel 28).

Others, who made up their minds to wait with patience, have better stories: Joseph had to wait twelve years before he became the assistant to Pharaoh and head of all Egypt (Genesis 37; 39–41).

David had to wait decades from the time he was

anointed king until the time he was finally crowned king over all the houses of Israel (1 Samuel 16; 2 Samuel 2).

Waiting and persevering seem to have an incredible value to God. His timing never seems to be as soon as mine—but He is so good and always faithful, just in a different way than my impatient heart wants Him to be.

Waiting proves (or disproves!) the strength of our hearts and our convictions. If we do it well, it strengthens our faith. It increases our capacity to long for heavenly answers instead of just being satisfied with earthly, immediate fixes.

His Promises

But those who trust in the LORD will find new strength.
 They will soar high on wings like eagles.
They will run and not grow weary.
 They will walk and not faint.

ISAIAH 40:31

The LORD is good to those who depend on him,
 to those who search for him.

LAMENTATIONS 3:25

We can rejoice, too, when we run into problems and trials, for we know that they help us develop endurance. And endurance develops strength of character, and character strengthens our confident hope of salvation.

ROMANS 5:3-4

AS TEMPTING
AS IT MAY BE...

Every day, we have twenty-four hours to invest our lives in what will matter for eternity, and more often than not, it is in the seemingly insignificant moments of our lives when nobility, civility, and graciousness must flow from our hearts. We will often be tempted to act in a manner that is harsh, impatient, unloving, judgmental of others, and quick to lash out when we feel attacked. Yet, the only way to overcome these temptations is to invest in our spiritual lives every day by spending time with the Source of all goodness and loving-kindness, the Lord Jesus Himself. Hebrews 1:3 (NIV) tells us that He is the exact representation of God—He speaks God's words, He shows His heart, He manifests His wisdom.

Jesus said, "Learn from me, for I am gentle and humble in heart" (Matthew 11:29, NIV). This seems to be my pondering of the year. Learn from Him. He didn't revile when He was reviled. He loved and gave grace to Peter when he fell. He washed 120 toes the night before He was crucified, serving those for whom He would die.

The more we regularly invest our hearts, our commitments, our faith, our love in our relationship to our Lord, the more our own hearts will be noble and pure. Each second, each moment, each day, seek to emulate His life, choosing to obey, against your feelings, those things He speaks to your heart in the privacy of your time with Him.

His Promises

Humble yourselves before the Lord, and he will lift you up in honor.

JAMES 4:10

The temptations in your life are no different from what others experience. And God is faithful. He will not allow the temptation to be more than you can stand. When you are tempted, he will show you a way out so that you can endure.

1 CORINTHIANS 10:13

True humility and fear of the LORD
lead to riches, honor, and long life.

PROVERBS 22:4

THE BUCK
STOPS HERE

We are called to give up our lives, as Jesus gave up His life for us, for the purpose of training, loving, and preparing our children for life—eternal life. Jesus had a pretty strong opinion about what we would face if we willingly put our children in harm's way! We are not mature Christians if we're seeking to get rid of the "burden" of having children by handing the training of them to others. It is our responsibility to care for our children's souls, presenting Jesus to them in hopes that they will choose to follow Him.

It seems that these days, women are not being taught that choices have consequences—that their children's hearts, minds, morals, and future lives are dependent on the vision and faithfulness of mothers in this generation.

"What does it profit a mom to gain the whole world and lose her children's souls?" (my paraphrase of Mark 8:36).

If mothers do not take initiative now to be personally responsible for their children, we will never see a future generation of adults with excellent character, biblical convictions, and leadership qualities. We will not have children who have learned that family is important, that marriage is of great value to God, and that we are responsible for the world hearing the truth in our generation.

And yet, these truths are foundational to society! There is no better use of our time than to pour our lives out for God, both within our homes and without.

His Promises

Get up, for it is your duty to tell us how to proceed in setting things straight. We are behind you, so be strong and take action.

EZRA 10:4

And you should imitate me, just as I imitate Christ. I am so glad that you always keep me in your thoughts, and that you are following the teachings I passed on to you.

1 CORINTHIANS 11:1-2

Work hard so you can present yourself to God and receive his approval. Be a good worker, one who does not need to be ashamed and who correctly explains the word of truth.

2 TIMOTHY 2:15

CAN YOU HEAR ME NOW?

What are the messages you play over and over in your heart and mind? Your life will reflect the voices you are listening to and the messages you are believing and rehearsing.

If you feel condemned, inadequate, or judged, perhaps you are hearing that God is disappointed with you or that He is a God ready to condemn, a rule keeper—expecting more of you than you can give.

If you live in bitterness or anger, you are listening to voices that say life is unfair to you and God has not heard your prayers. Or perhaps you believe that no one really loves you and He is not really good.

On the other hand, if you are living with a real sense of His love and goodness, perhaps you are listening to messages that say, "There is now no condemnation for those who are in Christ Jesus" (Romans 8:1, NIV). Or perhaps this one: "As a father has compassion on his children, so the LORD has compassion on those who fear Him" (Psalm 103:13, NIV).

Maybe you are living in hope and peace of mind, and the message in your heart is, "We know that God causes all things to work together for good to those who love God, to those who are called according to His purpose" (Romans 8:28, NASB). Or it could be, "I know whom I have believed and I am convinced that He is able to guard what I have entrusted to Him until that day" (2 Timothy 1:12, NASB).

You are what you believe, and your actions show those beliefs to the world.

His Promises

Because of the privilege and authority God has given me, I give each of you this warning: Don't think you are better than you really are. Be honest in your evaluation of yourselves, measuring yourselves by the faith God has given us.

ROMANS 12:3

Examine yourselves to see if your faith is genuine. Test yourselves. Surely you know that Jesus Christ is among you; if not, you have failed the test of genuine faith.

2 CORINTHIANS 13:5

You made all the delicate, inner parts of my body
*   and knit me together in my mother's womb.*
Thank you for making me so wonderfully complex!
*   Your workmanship is marvelous—how well I know it.*

PSALM 139:13-14

LESS IS MORE

God's will is very clear and straightforward—rejoice, pray, and give thanks in everything. A heart that is grateful is a heart that is satisfied and content.

At this juncture in history, we have more material goods, more entertainment, and more food options than at any other time. Yet, "having more" has created a culture that is never satisfied, often in debt, and dependent on self-gratification while neglecting the greater needs of people less fortunate than themselves. Children are coddled, entertained to death, and spoiled with expectations that can never totally be assuaged, which creates a complaining spirit and self-pity if every desire is not promptly met.

Worse, many parents have come to think they are supposed to provide all these things for their children so they can be happy, instead of understanding God wants them to cultivate children who have learned to be content.

Jesus came into the world with no stately form

or majesty that would cause us to look upon Him. Having no title, and few possessions, He chose fishermen, tax collectors, and common men and women to be His companions. He lived a simple, common life, with "nowhere to lay His head." In this, He modeled to us a thankful heart.

Simplicity is one of the keys to gratitude. For children, how important it is that they learn to be satisfied with playing at the beach or walking in a forest or digging in the dirt, carrying a notebook around so they can draw a tree or flowers, singing and dreaming under a shade tree.

His Promises

Don't love money; be satisfied with what you have.
*   For God has said,*
*   "I will never fail you.*
I will never abandon you."

HEBREWS 13:5

Yet true godliness with contentment is itself great wealth. After all, we brought nothing with us when we came into the world, and we can't take anything with us when we leave it. So if we have enough food and clothing, let us be content.

1 TIMOTHY 6:6-8

And this same God who takes care of me will supply all your needs from his glorious riches, which have been given to us in Christ Jesus.

PHILIPPIANS 4:19

WORTH
FIGHTING FOR

In Genesis 1, we read that God created the heavens and the earth, and it was good. We can see the handiwork of the Lord—the intricacy of design—from snowflakes to zebras, an iris to a mimosa tree—all of this speaks to the magnificence of our transcendent Creator God.

Family was thought up by God to give all people a place to belong. The family and home were to be a haven—a place where celebration would take place; a port in the midst of the storms where one could come for peace, strength, help, and security; a place of comfort amidst the demands and stresses of life. The rhythm of eating together, playing together, working together, and loving together was to be a circle of God's presence.

A mother and father were to be the inspirational leaders, providers, teachers, counselors, cheerleaders, spiritual guides, and friends to usher their children through life with emotional, physical, and spiritual health.

It is no wonder that Satan has sought to break up the family. If a person is isolated from all support and love and accountability that God intended to be his strength and foundation through his family, then he will be an easy target for the enemy.

A family, a home, a heritage is all worth fighting for—it is God's design, it is His way, the way of His best blessing—even in a fallen world—worth the cost for a future that is secure.

His Promises

Those who live in the shelter of the Most High
  will find rest in the shadow of the Almighty.
This I declare about the LORD:
  He alone is my refuge, my place of safety;
he is my God, and I trust him.

PSALM 91:1-2

Therefore, since we have been made right in God's sight by faith, we have peace with God because of what Jesus Christ our Lord has done for us.

ROMANS 5:1

Having hope will give you courage.
  You will be protected and will rest in safety.

JOB 11:18

COMMUNITY
SPIRIT

Sometimes we are so intent on keeping our heads down and our hands to the plow that we don't even recognize our need for other women. In days of old, people were born into and lived in their communities their whole lives. They knew their neighbors, and when they hung the laundry out to dry, they chatted over the fence with them. When they needed to borrow a cup of sugar, they went next door to that same friend they had known for years. Parents often lived in the same house as their adult children, and aunts and uncles and cousins would live nearby too.

Now, we live apart. Many of us attend churches of thousands, which are not in our neighborhoods. We don't usually know our neighbors, and we often have no values or background in common with those neighbors, anyway. So, we become used to fending for ourselves, until eventually we find ourselves exhausted, wanting to give up, and wondering where God has gone.

God's design was always for us to live in community. The family was to be a large group living together, loving each other, and sharing life and traditions together. There would be lots of children with similar values and close relationships, so moms could actually have a few minutes alone while the children played and ran and had wholesome fun.

No wonder Satan works so hard at creating isolation among us—because when we are alone in our homes, we naturally compromise our ideals, become discouraged, and listen to his voice of discouragement.

His Promises

If one part suffers, all the parts suffer with it, and if one part is honored, all the parts are glad.

All of you together are Christ's body, and each of you is a part of it.

1 CORINTHIANS 12:26-27

But if we are living in the light, as God is in the light, then we have fellowship with each other, and the blood of Jesus, his Son, cleanses us from all sin.

1 JOHN 1:7

I appeal to you, dear brothers and sisters, by the authority of our Lord Jesus Christ, to live in harmony with each other. Let there be no divisions in the church. Rather, be of one mind, united in thought and purpose.

1 CORINTHIANS 1:10

STAY
THE COURSE!

God's Word is clear: He values dedication and perseverance, as they are part of His own character.

Yet, daily, people are tempted to give up on their ideals—giving up in marriage, in relationships, on a child, on a commitment. People capitulate all the time to Satan's wily and clever messages encouraging them to compromise—"You can't expect anyone in this time of the world to be moral. No one else is doing this hard thing you're doing. You deserve better than this."

There are so many messages he sends to try and make us want to quit. However, if we persevere and wait on God, we will receive the reward of a holier character and the grace of seeing Him work in our lives.

So, today, if you are weary, discouraged, or down-hearted, look up—God sees you, God is at work. Don't quit before He accomplishes His will. You will be greatly fulfilled if you keep going and wait for God's grace and for His work in His way at His time. When

I look back, I see His wisdom and how He was always in control—even when it didn't seem like He was.

His Promises

Therefore, since we are surrounded by such a huge crowd of witnesses to the life of faith, let us strip off every weight that slows us down, especially the sin that so easily trips us up. And let us run with endurance the race God has set before us. We do this by keeping our eyes on Jesus, the champion who initiates and perfects our faith. Because of the joy awaiting him, he endured the cross, disregarding its shame. Now he is seated in the place of honor beside God's throne.

    HEBREWS 12:1-2

If you look for me wholeheartedly, you will find me.

    JEREMIAH 29:13

And I am certain that God, who began the good work within you, will continue his work until it is finally finished on the day when Christ Jesus returns.

    PHILIPPIANS 1:6

NO TIME LIKE
THE PRESENT

When I had little babies, I had the illusion that some-day, life would settle down and I would have more personal time to myself. Most moms find themselves saying, "Life will be easier when . . . the baby sleeps through the night/there aren't any more babies/all are out of diapers/all are reading/all can drive/all are through with these hormonal teen years . . ."

Yet, if we are not careful, we can fritter life away waiting for an elusive time in the future when we think all will be well and we will have more time to read, have quiet times, savor moments with our children, be sensitive to our husband's needs, or pray about what is on the heart of Jesus.

By doing that, we miss living today to its fullest and for God's glory. We miss the life that was the will of God.

We would all agree that we do not want to live the Martha life—always busy, busy, busy and a tad upset and grumpy, feeling sorry for ourselves, overwhelmed with the lists, having negative thoughts about our children, husband, and life. We do not always take the time to evaluate and see ourselves as we really are.

Mary dropped everything she had to do, sat at Jesus' feet, engaged her heart, listened intently, and worshiped. She was seeking and choosing what Martha was too distracted and busy to choose. There is evidently only one good path to choose, and it would not be taken away from Mary since she chose it.

His Promises

We also pray that you will be strengthened with all his glorious power so you will have all the endurance and patience you need. May you be filled with joy, always thanking the Father.

COLOSSIANS 1:11

Teach us to realize the brevity of life,
so that we may grow in wisdom.

PSALM 90:12

Don't worry about tomorrow, for tomorrow will bring its own worries. Today's trouble is enough for today.

MATTHEW 6:34

A BREED APART

We don't hear it very often, but the Bible is clear that God wants us to walk in holiness. So what does it mean to be holy—set apart for God?

It means we have learned to view our lives in light of eternity. It is to live by scriptural principles— seeking first the Kingdom of God, laying up treasures in heaven and not on earth, numbering our days to present God with a heart of wisdom, loving God and our neighbors.

We must put away the sin inside our hearts. We need to root out idols in our lives, anything that we look to for our primary source of value or joy, whether money, television, social media, food, popularity, or any areas of sin we have not repented of.

Holiness means we must spend time in His Word. A holy person is humble: meek, compassionate, and gracious to others. We must be committed to grow- ing in love, because this is what pleases God. Loving means putting away anger and harshness and seeing the other person through the eyes of serving and encouraging them, not looking for what the person can do for me.

Holiness requires us to believe in God's presence, purpose, and attention, every moment, every day. Without faith, it is impossible to please Him. We believe during the dark times of life. We worship and sing to Him every day. We wait as long as it takes to see His answer to our prayers. We wait on God and God only.

His Promises

Work at living in peace with everyone, and work at living a holy life, for those who are not holy will not see the Lord.

HEBREWS 12:14

Jesus told him, "I am the way, the truth, and the life. No one can come to the Father except through me."

JOHN 14:6

But now you must be holy in everything you do, just as God who chose you is holy. For the Scriptures say, "You must be holy because I am holy."

1 PETER 1:15-16

TIME OUT

If you find yourself snapping at your children or feeling upset with someone over petty things, it may be because you haven't had enough time with God. Without the investment of time with Jesus, it is impossible to be spiritual!

Here are a few practical suggestions for meeting with God:

1. **Find a time (or times) you can set aside to meet with God.** Even five minutes is better than nothing! There is no specific time more holy than others—you can learn just as much at midnight as you can at early dawn.

2. **Read through the Psalms, one each day.** Circle or write down any truth it teaches you about God.

3. **Do the same with the book of Hebrews.** Look at Hebrews to learn the lessons of what pleases God, the attributes of Jesus, and His will for us to hold fast.

4. **Read a chapter of Proverbs each day** and keep a list of what this book teaches you about folly versus wisdom.

Allow me to pray for you as you seek to regularly meet with God.

Lord, I pray that You will raise up women who will love You, seek You, trust You, and serve You with their whole hearts. Speak to them in their needs and issues of life and help them to learn from You. Comfort them and guide them in wisdom. Bless these precious ones, I pray, and thank You so much for Your generous, unfailing love. We love and worship You. In Jesus' precious and wonderful name we come. Amen.

His Promises

Come close to God, and God will come close to you.
JAMES 4:8

I have hidden your word in my heart,
that I might not sin against you.
PSALM 119:11

Those who live in the shelter of the Most High
will find rest in the shadow of the Almighty.
PSALM 91:1

YOU ARE
THE KEY!

Everyone wants to know just what to do to have good results with their children, yet there is no one-size-fits-all answer. There is, however, one important key: you! The key to raising excellent children is for you to grow in excellence. You cannot give your children what you do not possess. Buying the best curriculum or the most expensive lessons cannot compensate for shortcomings in your own life; as the Scripture says, your children will be like their teacher. We, as teachers and models, do not need to condemn ourselves for not being perfect. Yet, even as we look for a heart of obedience in our children, a willingness to try to please us, so He is looking for that intention in us.

You can always accomplish more than you thought with God at your side. God's grace carries you through each weakness, failure, and sin, but He is always calling you to live beyond the place where you are, to grow more fully into the you He created you to be. If you are growing, learning, loving more, living more intentionally, He will bring excellence and growth into the very fiber of your family life. For indeed, the most important resource to your children in their life education is you, as you submit to God's training and calling on your own life, fully committed to being like Him, your Teacher.

His Promises

I will teach all your children,
and they will enjoy great peace.
ISAIAH 54:13

But you must remain faithful to the things you have been taught. You know they are true, for you know you can trust those who taught you. You have been taught the holy Scriptures from childhood, and they have given you the wisdom to receive the salvation that comes by trusting in Christ Jesus.
2 TIMOTHY 3:14-15

Let each generation tell its children of your mighty acts;
let them proclaim your power.
PSALM 145:4

FOLLOW
THE LEADERS

God promises that He will support us, give us strength, and help us know how to take action. Many people in the Bible—including Esther, Daniel, David, Moses, Abraham, Ruth, Peter, and Mary, the mother of Jesus—displayed strength and took action in their own times. These are our models who give us hope to think that all of us, when filled with the Spirit of God, might do the same.

How do you move in the direction of receiving God's strength?

1. **Find those who, when you are with them, cause you to want to be better and more faithful and who inspire you to walk with God.** Whether in books, or in person, do what you can to be with them.
2. **Read biographies of faith-oriented people God has used.** Corrie ten Boom, Brother Andrew, Amy Carmichael, Hudson Taylor, George Müller, Ben Carson, Andrew Carnegie,

Mother Teresa, Jim Elliot—there are so many who are inspiring because they were moved to take action in their generations.

3. **To know God, you must invest in His Word and prayer.** You could not deeply know someone with whom you never communicated. The more you are with God, the more you will reflect His influence.

4. **Regularly get away by yourself and observe the details of your life.** What is draining you? Where have you ceased to believe God? Is there any sin habit that is building an invisible wall between you and God? What activities are necessary, and which might be dropped?

His Promises

Remember your leaders who taught you the word of God. Think of all the good that has come from their lives, and follow the example of their faith.

HEBREWS 13:7

And the Holy Spirit helps us in our weakness. For example, we don't know what God wants us to pray for. But the Holy Spirit prays for us with groanings that cannot be expressed in words.

ROMANS 8:26

Ask me and I will tell you remarkable secrets you do not know about things to come.

JEREMIAH 33:3

WHEN THE GOING GETS TOUGH...

As godly mothers, we strive to make the best possible decisions, set the perfect boundaries, and uphold the correct rules, which we believe will somehow cultivate spiritual children. However, there is a mysterious process by which the Holy Spirit leads our children to see their need for Christ even as we seek to cultivate their hearts.

We put *so* much pressure on ourselves as mothers. Each time we find ourselves too busy to cook, too exhausted to clean, or so hectic in our lives that we didn't do a devotional with our children one week, we feel defeated and believe that we failed.

The truth is, the grace of God is given in spite of our circumstances. His peace comes when our difficulties would suggest otherwise.

While it is wonderful to set our standards high and live within these great ideals, we must hold ourselves to a standard of *grace*, not perfection. We won't be able to have grace for our children if we do not have grace for ourselves.

His Promises

Don't worry about anything; instead, pray about everything. Tell God what you need, and thank him for all he has done. Then you will experience God's peace, which exceeds anything we can understand. His peace will guard your hearts and minds as you live in Christ Jesus.

PHILIPPIANS 4:6-7

You will keep in perfect peace
    all who trust in you,
all whose thoughts are fixed on you!

ISAIAH 26:3

I pray that God, the source of hope, will fill you completely with joy and peace because you trust in him. Then you will overflow with confident hope through the power of the Holy Spirit.

ROMANS 15:13

YOU GET OUT
WHAT YOU PUT IN

When you are taxed by your children, your friends, or your husband, what flows out from the depths of your heart? Filling our souls with beauty, goodness, humility, faith, and the love of Christ must be intentional so His life will be what spills over onto others when we are "squeezed."

Jesus said it is not the outside—our performance for others or attempts to do righteous works—that determines what a man or woman is like. It is possible to fool others because of our behavior, but it is never possible to fool God. He sees what we are like on the inside.

The starting point for spreading inspiration and faith is cultivating our own hearts. If a mama is reading Scripture, pondering the heart of Christ, worshiping Him, and following His ways, her children will draw the love and sweetness of Christ from her every day.

If a mama is engaging her mind in great books,

learning new ideas, and stretching her own intellect, her children will also benefit.

If a mama is developing her character and taking small steps to become more self-disciplined, more of a servant leader, more patient, and more generous with lifegiving words because of her obedience to Christ, her children's souls will be watered by the strength of her obedience.

If she engages herself in meeting the needs of others and reaches out with the redeeming message of Christ, her children will learn not just to hear words of the gospel, but to live the gospel.

His Promises

He renews my strength.
He guides me along right paths,
bringing honor to his name.

PSALM 23:3

Jesus replied, "All who love me will do what I say. My Father will love them, and we will come and make our home with each of them.

JOHN 14:23

He will cover you with his feathers.
He will shelter you with his wings.
His faithful promises are your armor and protection.

PSALM 91:4

NO PROBLEM TOO BIG OR TOO SMALL

Hope is not just wishful thinking. Hope is an assurance that our King has ultimately won the raging battle. When we have nothing else to rely on, our hope in God is what connects us to what is true.

Faith requires us to relinquish our fears, doubts, and worries into the hands of God, like a child who says, "I will trust my mama and daddy because I know they are good and reliable." So we say, "I will give this difficulty into His hands because I know He is good and loving and reliable."

Hope gives us the strength to take on our future. No circumstance, no problem, no issue, no devastation is too large or too difficult for God to take on. However, we have to *choose* this hope. We must receive it. Sometimes, life can beat us down and make us feel absolutely defeated. But when we choose to carry the hope God has given us, we are able to overcome *anything*.

Our hope rests in God's character and ability to see us through. In Him who answers prayer. In Him who is always good. In Him who has overcome the world. In Him who has forgiven every sin. In Him who will never leave us or forsake us. We can leave our issues in the file drawer of heaven and know that He has the ability to work them out and to cause "all things to work together for good to those who love God" (Romans 8:28, NASB).

His Promises

We were given this hope when we were saved. (If we already have something, we don't need to hope for it. But if we look forward to something we don't yet have, we must wait patiently and confidently.)

ROMANS 8:24-25

Faith shows the reality of what we hope for; it is the evidence of things we cannot see.

HEBREWS 11:1

All praise to God, the Father of our Lord Jesus Christ. It is by his great mercy that we have been born again, because God raised Jesus Christ from the dead. Now we live with great expectation.

1 PETER 1:3

HOLD TIGHT!

In a culture that has fast food, air travel, and nearly instantaneous responses to communication, the value of patience has become lost. Yet, patience is the virtue that will cause us to grow spiritually like no other. Waiting for our prayers to be answered forces us to look to God, to humble ourselves before Him, to acknowledge our dependence on Him.

God has wisdom, and He has a plan. He works to build spiritual muscle slowly, because His focus is on building character and the likeness of Christ in our lives. Holiness does not come from a quick fix.

If we are to resist evil and overcome it with good, we must learn the value of waiting patiently in the midst of life's storms. Weeping is for the night, but joy comes in the morning, as the psalms say.

All of life in a fallen world requires us to be patient and to rule over our impatient spirits. We do not walk by emotions or whims, but we learn to walk in obedience to the path God has given. Then, His reward will be sure and generous.

The value of training and teaching our children to put off self-gratification is great. Gently helping them to choose patience, to will to be strong, to wait on God, is to prepare them to understand how to live their lives for Him rather than themselves.

His Promises

Be on guard. Stand firm in the faith. Be courageous. Be strong.

1 CORINTHIANS 16:13

For God has not given us a spirit of fear and timidity, but of power, love, and self-discipline.

2 TIMOTHY 1:7

For I know the plans I have for you," says the LORD. "They are plans for good and not for disaster, to give you a future and a hope."

JEREMIAH 29:11

PLAY TIME

Too often today, children are starving for real life and drowning in the midst of an empty one.

When they are constantly using technology for entertainment, children's brains have been shown to slow down because they are overstimulated, and their undeveloped eyes and brains cannot process what they are taking in. Children need to be outdoors. They need time to be bored. They need to be around books, have lots and lots of imaginative stories read to them, and then have time to act out the stories. They need lots of time with adults so that they can pattern their values and manners and relationships after mature people rather than always being in the company of immature children or exposed to digital images that display violence, foolishness, and questionable values.

May all children be blessed with the gift of play, imagination, free time, and the space to be outdoors to explore. May they wonder at the marvels of God's creation. May they have the treasure of real human beings who hold their hands while they explore the world, who rock them to sleep and sing them real songs and scratch their backs at bedtime and tell them their own love stories. And may they daily hear the words of their Creator God, marvel at His excellence, and grow to love Him with all of their hearts.

His Promises

There is nothing better than to enjoy food and drink and to find satisfaction in work. Then I realized that these pleasures are from the hand of God.

ECCLESIASTES 2:24

You will show me the way of life,
granting me the joy of your presence
and the pleasures of living with you forever.

PSALM 16:11

This is the day the LORD has made.
We will rejoice and be glad in it.

PSALM 118:24

SOLID
GROUND

Negative attitudes of the heart—whining, complaining, discouragement, defeatism—can affect our ability to endure. Endurance requires the habit of faith, which you can intentionally train in your children.

One of the best and most delightful ways you can teach your children what enduring faith looks like is to read stories about heroism. Read to your children stories of biblical heroes, of missionaries, of historical people who lived their whole lives with an enduring faith in God. For Christian stories, we loved the *Hero Tales* series by Dave and Neta Jackson. We also read books about William Wilberforce, Abraham Lincoln, and many other historical figures—men and women who influenced their generations in heroic ways. We read biographies of great scientists, artists, inventors, explorers, statesmen, and teachers who endured with faith in order to change the world through their lives. Every story you read with your children feeds their imagination of what it looks like to be brave, to be gracious, to endure hardship, and to win the race. Encouragement also helps your children endure by faith; positive words will narrate steadfastness into their lives. Instead of lecturing your discouraged child, or verbalizing disappointment, articulate your belief in them. "I believe you can do this. I can't wait to see what God does with your life. I'm so proud of you. Keep trying. You're getting to be so strong. Don't give up." Your words of affirmation will become solid ground they can stand on to take the next step.

His Promises

The LORD is my strength and shield.
  I trust him with all my heart.
He helps me, and my heart is filled with joy.
  I burst out in songs of thanksgiving.

  PSALM 28:7

Most important of all, continue to show deep love for each other, for love covers a multitude of sins. Cheerfully share your home with those who need a meal or a place to stay. God has given each of you a gift from his great variety of spiritual gifts. Use them well to serve one another.

  1 PETER 4:8-10

Brothers and sisters, we urge you to warn those who are lazy. Encourage those who are timid. Take tender care of those who are weak. Be patient with everyone.

  1 THESSALONIANS 5:14

PUTTING OTHERS FIRST

We all know what it is like to be around a whiner or selfish person who has to be treated specially, whose needs must always be met for them to be happy.

How do we teach our children to give up their belongings, their time, their lives to others?

1. **Teach your children to share and help one another from the very beginning.** "You are such a strong boy, and I can see your sister needs your help. Would you please help her carry her box of toys to her room?"

2. **Teach your children Bible stories and hero stories about those who gave, such as the little boy who gave his lunch so Jesus could feed the five thousand.** Show your children that Jesus looked out on the crowd and had compassion, and say, "I wonder who needs our compassion. Let's look out for people

God brings our way to encourage or to give something to."

3. **Plan real ways for them to give and share.** Have them give up their rooms when company comes and sleep on the floor of your bedroom. Then praise them, of course! Let praying for, loving, encouraging, and serving others be the oxygen of your home.

Teaching them to live like this takes years and lots of time and planning, but you will give them the gift of an unselfish heart that serves and character that will give them contentment and self-control for the rest of their lives.

His Promises

But be sure to fear the LORD and faithfully serve him. Think of all the wonderful things he has done for you.

1 SAMUEL 12:24

As for the rest of you, dear brothers and sisters, never get tired of doing good.

2 THESSALONIANS 3:13

Give, and you will receive. Your gift will return to you in full—pressed down, shaken together to make room for more, running over, and poured into your lap. The amount you give will determine the amount you get back.

LUKE 6:38

LET THERE BE LIGHT

The first words of God in the Bible are "Let there be light" (Genesis 1:3), for without light, there is no life. David says, "The LORD is my light and my salvation" (Psalm 27:1), the One who saves his life. Jesus, the incarnate Son of God, proclaims, "I am the Light of the world; he who follows Me will not walk in the darkness, but will have the Light of life" (John 8:12, NASB).

So when we give our children God's life, we are also giving them His light. It is the light of God that will shine in our hearts and our homes so that we can be a beacon of hope to the world around us. Lifegiving parenting must first be about helping them find eternal life in Christ and getting them on God's path so they can live in a way that's pleasing to Him. On a much grander scale, lifegiving parenting is about writing ourselves and our children into the overarching story of God's eternal plan. His life and light are what make us "the light of the world" so that we can "shine before men in such a way that they may see [our] good works and glorify [our] Father who is in heaven" (Matthew 5:14-16, NASB). It's about turning on that light in our homes so others who are overcome by darkness may see it and find the light and life in Christ that we have found.

His Promises

I am the light of the world. If you follow me, you won't have to walk in darkness, because you will have the light that leads to life.

JOHN 8:12

The light shines in the darkness,
    and the darkness can never extinguish it.

JOHN 1:5

For once you were full of darkness, but now you have light from the Lord. So live as people of light!

EPHESIANS 5:8

LOSING CONTROL

We humans are complex creatures, shaped internally by drives, fears, pride, ideals, hopes, and other unseen but influential forces.

Even though we are new creatures in Christ, we are still tempted by our sinful nature. And if we let emotions control us, strong feelings can affect how we interact with our immature children. Emotion-filled reactions such as anger, judgment, or criticism can replace thoughtful and reasoned actions. Also, we can let fear—of what others think, of doing the wrong thing, of angering God—control us.

Those negative human forces, and many more, can influence our parenting, but only if we let them. The good news is that we have a choice; we can learn to let God be in control of our parenting. We can let Him become the controlling influence in our lives so our children will see the new person we are becoming in Christ, not the old person we were before. That happens through three positive influences by which God comes into our humanity—faith, freedom, and love. Much of parenting is simply learning to "walk by faith, not by sight" (2 Corinthians 5:7, NASB)—trusting in God for His wisdom, insight, and discernment to become the Christlike parents our children need. Faith, then, gives us the freedom to follow the Holy Spirit's ministry in our hearts and not be enslaved to man's laws and rules.

His Promises

Fools vent their anger,
*   but the wise quietly hold it back.*

PROVERBS 29:11

Better to be patient than powerful;
*   better to have self-control than to conquer a city.*

PROVERBS 16:32

Make every effort to supplement your faith with
virtue, and virtue with knowledge, and knowledge with
self-control, and self-control with steadfastness, and
steadfastness with godliness.

2 PETER 1:5-6, ESV

YOU ARE
NOT ALONE

Committed motherhood is a holy calling of God. You are a steward of the children He has given you, and He trusts you to love, instruct, train, and provide for them in such a way that they may go into their adult lives emotionally healthy, loving God and serving His Kingdom purposes.

However, like most mothers, there are likely times when the work of giving, serving, cleaning, cooking, and correcting causes frustration to build up inside until it suddenly takes over and spills anger on everyone in close range.

When that happens, you do not need a lecture from someone telling you you've been immature, out of control, unreasonable, or unloving. You already know that. What you long for instead is gentleness and patience—someone to tenderly place their arms around your shoulders, look into your eyes with compassion, understand how you feel, and say, "Grace to you, sweet one; you are forgiven. All will be well."

As one mom to another, let me assure you, you are not the only mother to lose her patience. I am guilty of raging in the tempests of my own life too. Apologize, ask forgiveness, and move on in love. So the next time life overwhelms you and you lose it with your children, remember, you're not alone, and it's not irreparable. Apologize honestly. Ask forgiveness. Begin again. God has already forgiven you and provided for a new tomorrow.

His Promises

Confess your sins to each other and pray for each other so that you may be healed. The earnest prayer of a righteous person has great power and produces wonderful results.

JAMES 5:16

Work at living in peace with everyone, and work at living a holy life, for those who are not holy will not see the Lord. Look after each other so that none of you fails to receive the grace of God. Watch out that no poisonous root of bitterness grows up to trouble you, corrupting many.

HEBREWS 12:14-15

But if we confess our sins to him, he is faithful and just to forgive us our sins and to cleanse us from all wickedness.

1 JOHN 1:9

WORD TO
THE WISE

Jesus was (and is) the Word—the message that brought life to those who were thirsty, love to those who felt unlovable, truth to those who longed for direction, comfort to those who were weary, forgiveness to those who were guilty.

Words have power to destroy or to heal. Even Peter, with all of his blunderings, got this right: "Lord, to whom shall we go? You have words of eternal life" (John 6:68, NASB).

Jesus said, "Out of the abundance of the heart his mouth speaks" (Luke 6:45, ESV).

Remember, "the Word," Jesus, lives inside you. That means you have the power within to cultivate that which will bring the same life and truth that He brought. That is why you should spend more time pondering His words, His heart, His messages— so you can be changed by them.

Make it a habit to begin each day saying, "Today,

I am going to be intentional about my words. I will write or speak words of life intentionally to each of my children today—face to face or on messages they will receive. I hope to hearten them, lift them, encourage them. I will invest words that my husband needs to hear. I will seek this week to give out those words to people He brings to my mind, that they might feel the wind of the Holy Spirit blowing through their lives."

May your words cause all who are around you to sense the fragrance of God lingering about them.

His Promises

But Jesus told him, "No! The Scriptures say, 'People do not live by bread alone,
but by every word that comes from the mouth of God.'"
MATTHEW 4:4

It is the same with my word.
I send it out, and it always produces fruit.
It will accomplish all I want it to,
and it will prosper everywhere I send it.
ISAIAH 55:11

Jesus replied, "But even more blessed are all who hear the word of God and put it into practice."
LUKE 11:28

DOWN, BUT
NOT OUT

When we find ourselves in difficult circumstances, especially in seasons where trouble seems to come in waves, we see ourselves for what we really are. Our souls are laid bare. Our limitations, vulnerability, and weaknesses are exposed, as well as our inability to do anything to save ourselves.

The situation for each one might be different: a broken marriage, a prodigal or otherwise seemingly impossible child, financial issues, loneliness, failure, broken dreams. Whatever the situation, we feel alone, unnoticed, helpless.

Of course, this is the place where God can teach us to rely on Him completely. He so desires to be the One who fulfills our greatest longings. He wants us to know His voice of guidance, purpose, love, and mercy.

It seems those who are wisest, most true, and deepest in humility and gentleness have had to walk through many such times of doubt and testing. Because they have lived through those times, they are deeper, more aware of their need for God, more thankful for His mercy, more focused on eternity, more compassionate toward those who are lost, and more humble in their demeanor.

Sometimes, in all of our efforts to control life and to accomplish our works, we subtly think our success depends on ourselves. Our happiness can be found by striving enough. A loving Father must bring us to the edge of our own limitations, so that we can live above our mere worldly focus and become more familiar with His strength and mercy and love and ways.

His Promises

Yes, I am the vine; you are the branches. Those who remain in me, and I in them, will produce much fruit. For apart from me you can do nothing.

JOHN 15:5

Blessed is the man who makes
the LORD his trust.

PSALM 40:4, ESV

This is what the Sovereign Lord,
the Holy One of Israel, says:
"Only in returning to me
and resting in me will you be saved.
In quietness and confidence is your strength."

ISAIAH 30:15

LETTING GO

Babies are dependent on us for their very existence—
our milk, our protection, our love and care, every
moment of every day. When we answer their cries
with tenderness and love, it helps them trust, and
eventually they relate to the idea that God is also One
who responds to their cries. In feeling our love, they
become predisposed to know and believe in His love
and touch when they hear stories about Him.

When we are new parents of young children, we
have a sense that we are in control of their lives—that
what we do and how we control them will determine
what they will become.

However, as our children grow, we realize we cannot control their lives or their circumstances, and they
must make their own decisions. There is a dark world
of temptation, idolatry, despair, and immorality calling to them at every point. But that does not mean we
are helpless. We can have a big impact on their lives
and help shoulder their burdens every day.

Consider how Jesus prayed specifically for Peter before he was tempted to deny Him, and reflect on the loving, tender words of prayer in John 17. We must model our lives after His. There is One who works directly within our children's hearts, One whose fingertips will mold and shape them: the Holy Spirit. Our work is to mysteriously engage with Him before God's throne, and it is there that the life of our children will bloom afresh.

His Promises

See, God has come to save me.
   I will trust in him and not be afraid.
The LORD God is my strength and my song;
   he has given me victory.

ISAIAH 12:2

I'm not asking you to take them out of the world, but to keep them safe from the evil one. They do not belong to this world any more than I do. Make them holy by your truth; teach them your word, which is truth. Just as you sent me into the world, I am sending them into the world. And I give myself as a holy sacrifice for them so they can be made holy by your truth.

JOHN 17:15-19

It is better to take refuge in the LORD
   than to trust in people.

PSALM 118:8

MUSCLE UP

Quitting jobs, quitting school, quitting on marriage, quitting on friendship, quitting on God—it seems all kinds of quitting have become acceptable and excusable these days.

Yet God gave us the capacity to "muscle up" in life, that we might be conquerors, defeat the darkness, and complete our work. How many times have you been tempted to give up on some of your ideals? How many times have your children tested your patience and faith and challenged you to the core? How often have work or financial issues tempted you to believe God did not hear your prayers? How often have people's negative voices caused you to second-guess your vision, tempting you to think ideals did not matter?

Daily life is where diligence is trained and learned. As our children watch our faithfulness and experience our love, they develop a heart to be diligent. Giving them work to complete develops moral strength.

Helping children to persevere in difficult relationships teaches them to be faithful in adult relationships.

Learning diligence is essential for fruitfulness. The world is in rebellion against God and His design, so our work is challenging, and our relationships are fraught with pain. But His spirit of redemption comes alive when we are diligent to complete the tasks we have been given. Diligence is the energy, the inner will of determination to keep going, that provides the power to overcome in life.

His Promises

So, my dear brothers and sisters, be strong and immovable. Always work enthusiastically for the Lord, for you know that nothing you do for the Lord is ever useless.

1 CORINTHIANS 15:58

Remember, it is sin to know what you ought to do and then not do it.

JAMES 4:17

If you love me, obey my commandments.

JOHN 14:15

YOU WERE MADE
FOR THIS

The glory of a woman is her ability to stir up life in this dark world. We are born to civilize, to encourage, to inspire, to heal. Women are most beautiful when they are engaged in sharing the reality of His life and love wherever they go.

As long as you keep your soul alive by dwelling in His presence, remembering the roles He plays in your life, as long as you cultivate and practice a heart of love, you can overcome the darkness—including all darkness in your own soul—here on earth. But love and beauty and faith must be cultivated daily, in His presence, looking for His reality, so that your heart will be filled with His truth and His overcoming goodness and redeeming light.

You were created to be an overcomer, an artist who leaves beauty, a counselor who brings peace, a type of magician who brings hope and laughter in the very midst of despair.

So, today, become a cocreator with Him who is the source of all that is beautiful and good, celebrating His reality into the midst of this puzzle that is called life.

The strength of any woman is built on a foundation of what she cherishes, practices, waters, cultivates. Love is there, waiting to strengthen—the soul of a great woman depends on His love flowing in and through every day.

His Promises

The faithful love of the LORD never ends!
  His mercies never cease.
Great is his faithfulness;
  his mercies begin afresh each morning.

LAMENTATIONS 3:22-23

Love never gives up, never loses faith, is always hopeful, and endures through every circumstance.

1 CORINTHIANS 13:7

Commit everything you do to the LORD.
  Trust him, and he will help you.

PSALM 37:5

WALKING
WITH GOD

If there was one legacy I could leave to women, it would be to help them think more biblically. When a woman knows Scripture—not just verses here and there taken out of context but a biblical understanding from Genesis to Revelation—she has more confidence and ease in her walk with God.

God makes it clear throughout Scripture that His priority is that we know Him and love Him with our whole heart and mind. And so the starting point for any arena in our lives must be God—our worship of Him and knowledge of Him, plus obedience coming from a heart that wants to please Him.

As we live the Christian life, God has given us a brain to think, a conscience to nudge our hearts, and most importantly, the Holy Spirit who lives inside of us to guide us. All He asks is that we live by faith in Him and dependence on Him. God always loves to lead us and work through us by faith in relationship to Him and what He is impressing us to do, within the beautiful design of our femininity and womanhood. That is why it is crucial that we are spending time in His presence and seeking to build a foundation of conviction on Scripture and knowledge of God.

His Promises

Heaven and earth will disappear, but my words will never disappear.

MATTHEW 24:35

So we must listen very carefully to the truth we have heard, or we may drift away from it.

HEBREWS 2:1

All Scripture is inspired by God and is useful to teach us what is true and to make us realize what is wrong in our lives. It corrects us when we are wrong and teaches us to do what is right.

2 TIMOTHY 3:16

RAISE YOUR HANDS

Often, we think of worship as singing, praising, and lifting our hands up to God. But while all these may be part of worship, to truly worship God means to honor Him and to place Him as the lens through which we see and live our lives.

We are told to worship Him with our mind. Filling our minds with truth, pondering Christ, cherishing that which is holy is a part of this worship. God admonishes us to delight ourselves in His law in Psalm 1, which indicates we need to hide His Word in our hearts and minds and think true thoughts.

We are told to think only on things that are worthy of Him: "Finally, brothers and sisters, whatever is true, whatever is noble, whatever is right, whatever is pure, whatever is lovely, whatever is admirable—if anything is excellent or praiseworthy—think about such things" (Philippians 4:8, NIV).

You cannot build your children into people who

seek to be worthy of God and to be excellent in all their ways, unless you also invest in their minds. The foundations of their thinking patterns, vocabulary, and ideas must be cultivated. When you become a steward of what they think, your own life is enriched. And so worshiping God with our minds requires commitment, planning, and intention.

If we are to be worthy stewards of truth, we must mind our minds—that we might truly worship.

His Promises

But the time is coming—indeed it's here now—when true worshipers will worship the Father in spirit and in truth. The Father is looking for those who will worship him that way. For God is Spirit, so those who worship him must worship in spirit and in truth.

JOHN 4:23-24

If you openly declare that Jesus is Lord and believe in your heart that God raised him from the dead, you will be saved.

ROMANS 10:9

Guard your heart above all else,
for it determines the course of your life.

PROVERBS 4:23

CHIN UP

Life is a constant challenge, every day, all the time. Things quit working, someone makes a mess, a situation just isn't fair. But what can make it worse is children and adults who whine and complain all the time. The habit of whining and complaining turns quickly into an attitude of self-absorption, which destroys hope, light, and beauty.

We have the opportunity to work with our children in hard or unfair situations to help them learn to be strong and mount up over their difficulties. This is what character training is all about—helping our children become stronger one day at a time. It is our will that chooses to have faith in God, that learns how to persevere under trial, that chooses to love the unlovely, that shows generosity to the needy. The will is what makes heroes, strong marriages, and legacies of faithfulness.

As we gently enter into the recesses of our children's

hearts and understand their feelings, we can then teach them to be strong inside, but with tender, grateful hearts. Our attitudes are the place where real strength and spirituality are expressed. When we approach our children with attitudes of gentleness and patience, we lead them to embrace these same patterns.

His Promises

We are pressed on every side by troubles, but we are not crushed. We are perplexed, but not driven to despair. We are hunted down, but never abandoned by God. We get knocked down, but we are not destroyed.

2 CORINTHIANS 4:8-9

I can do everything through Christ, who gives me strength.

PHILIPPIANS 4:13

In his kindness God called you to share in his eternal glory by means of Christ Jesus. So after you have suffered a little while, he will restore, support, and strengthen you, and he will place you on a firm foundation.

1 PETER 5:10

GRIDLOCK

All of us see our children through a grid. A grid is the lens through which we see life. It is created by what we are taught, what we experience, our own study, the surrounding culture, input from mentors, and hopefully prayer and the Holy Spirit! Our grid determines how we behave in relationship to our children.

Do you see your children through the grid of them being a blessing from God? To answer this question, consider this: How does one treat blessings and gifts?

We read in Mark 10:16 that Jesus took the little children into His arms and blessed them. Do you bless your children and see that as a part of being Jesus to them? He said of little children, "the kingdom of God belongs to such as these" (Luke 18:16, NASB).

It is written in Matthew 18:6 (NASB) that Jesus also said, "Whoever causes one of these little ones who believe in Me to stumble, it would be better for him to have a heavy millstone hung around his neck." What would cause a little one to stumble? I think this could include attitudes as well as actions. Are any of those things part of our lives?

As in all great work, raising godly children requires so very much time, effort, work, fortitude, faith, and patience. But it is such an important work, as it will last throughout eternity.

His Promises

Children are a gift from the LORD;
they are a reward from him.
Children born to a young man
are like arrows in a warrior's hands.
How joyful is the man whose quiver is full of them!

PSALM 127:3-5

Whatever is good and perfect is a gift coming down to us from God our Father, who created all the lights in the heavens.

JAMES 1:17

It will be like a woman suffering the pains of labor. When her child is born, her anguish gives way to joy because she has brought a new baby into the world.

JOHN 16:21

GROWING YOUR FAITH

Picture your soul as a garden that must be tended and cultivated and watered. If your soul is healthy, then those who draw from it will receive true nurture and strength. All great women of faith are very intentional about cultivating and building themselves into godly people. They invested purposefully to become who they are.

What are some ways to fill your own soul, so that you may have strength and love to give?

1. **Surround yourself with good and godly friends.** Find those friends: challenge a friend or two to be a prayer partner, to study a book together, or to meet with you on a regular basis.

2. **Spend time every day with the Lord. Find books, resources, people who can help you with this.** Some simple ways to do this: go

through Psalms and circle or underline every promise or character quality of God. Read one chapter of John or Matthew a day and write down one lesson you have learned. Read through Philippians and note all the ways Paul tells us to follow Jesus. You get the idea!

3. **Clean out your soul on a regular basis.**
Get rid of rubbish that has kept you from experiencing God's love. "If we confess our sins, He is faithful and righteous to forgive us our sins and to cleanse us from all unrighteousness" (1 John 1:9, NASB). Don't hang on to bitterness or condemnation—it will poison you. We must rid our hearts from lies that would keep us from experiencing the generous love of God.

His Promises

You must grow in the grace and knowledge of our Lord and Savior Jesus Christ.
All glory to him, both now and forever! Amen.

2 PETER 3:18

We ask God to give you complete knowledge of his will and to give you spiritual wisdom and understanding. Then the way you live will always honor and please the Lord, and your lives will produce every kind of good fruit. All the while, you will grow as you learn to know God better and better.

COLOSSIANS 1:9-10

Oh, the joys of those who do not
follow the advice of the wicked,
or stand around with sinners,
or join in with mockers.
But they delight in the law of the Lord,
meditating on it day and night.
They are like trees planted along the riverbank,
bearing fruit each season.
Their leaves never wither,
and they prosper in all they do.

PSALM 1:1-3

SOUL CARE

The only way you can be a loving mother, wife, or friend is to have your soul filled with the deep, unchanging, unconditional love of God.

So, how do you fill and enrich your soul?

1. **Be careful what you read! Surround yourself with books, blogs, and magazines that feed your mind on truth and encourage you to become a better self.** There are so many wonderful devotionals and autobiographies and classic fiction books that are encouraging and truthful, in contrast to others that stir feelings of insecurity or greed or even impurity. Choose well.

2. **Spend time in nature—His workshop.** When I see the artistry of God and rest in the glory of the canopy of His beauty, I find great peace. Creation was made for us. When I invest time in His works of art, I am inspired

to reflect His art and beauty in my home as a picture of His reality in an otherwise dark world. Creation nurtures my soul when I take time to observe it.

3. **Restore, relax, recreate.** Moms need sleep! Sometimes grumpiness or depression goes away with just a couple good nights of sleep or time away with a friend. Moms need to have a friend who understands them and still loves them! They need to laugh and lighten up. Cultivate times of breaks in your life, times of just getting away. Don't always be serious—it is exhausting.

His Promises

And now, just as you accepted Christ Jesus as your Lord, you must continue to follow him. Let your roots grow down into him, and let your lives be built on him. Then your faith will grow strong in the truth you were taught, and you will overflow with thankfulness.

COLOSSIANS 2:6-7

We will no longer be immature like children. We won't be tossed and blown about by every wind of new teaching. We will not be influenced when people try to trick us with lies so clever they sound like the truth. Instead, we will speak the truth in love, growing in every way more and more like Christ, who is the head of his body, the church.

EPHESIANS 4:14-15

So all of us who have had that veil removed can see and reflect the glory of the Lord. And the Lord—who is the Spirit—makes us more and more like him as we are changed into his glorious image.

2 CORINTHIANS 3:18

THINK SMALL

We want so much to give our lives to the "bigger" cause. We want to invest our lives for what is important. And yet, is there anything more important than the building of a righteous soul?

The laying down of our lives is not just about moving to the most impoverished country or preaching to thousands but loving the one right in front of us: the child who would long to have our comforting touch and gentle voice speaking lifegiving words, that he may imagine the voice and touch of God.

The child who needs one more song to be comforted before sleeping, so that he might be able to believe in a God who is patient and willing to answer prayer.

The child who is lonely, confused, and hormonal who will feel the sacrifice of God as we give up the rights to our personal time to listen and show compassion for what is on her heart.

Love is given through serving a special breakfast on Sunday before church as we open the gospel together, giving up what we wanted to do in order to build a soul, and looking into a child's eyes with true interest and compassion instead of looking at a screen while only half-listening. These are the sacrifices of our love, the moment-by-moment giving up of ourselves, the constant year-in, year-out practice of worship as we serve those in our home in order to please His heart.

His Promises

My old self has been crucified with Christ. It is no longer I who live, but Christ lives in me. So I live in this earthly body by trusting in the Son of God, who loved me and gave himself for me.

GALATIANS 2:20

If any of you wants to be my follower, you must give up your own way, take up your cross, and follow me. If you try to hang on to your life, you will lose it. But if you give up your life for my sake, you will save it.

MATTHEW 16:24-25

If you fully obey the LORD your God and carefully keep all his commands that I am giving you today, the LORD your God will set you high above all the nations of the world. You will experience all these blessings if you obey the LORD your God.

DEUTERONOMY 28:1-2

A LIGHT
IN THE DARK

There are times when it appears that all light, all hope, all strength, all answers are seeping out of our lives and we can do nothing to stop the darkness from coming. We are tempted to think that we cannot go one step more. We may even think that the Lord has abandoned us.

God led Abraham into the wilderness, where he was asked to sacrifice his only, beloved son—the one for whom he had waited years and years.

Joseph was brought unjustly into prison where he remained for years after being falsely accused of immorality by a devious woman.

Moses kept sheep and wandered the wilderness for forty years before he became the one who would lead the nation of Israel out of slavery.

Even Jesus was led into the wilderness to be tempted.

There is a mysterious value from heaven's point of

view to being in the darkness of life and still choosing to believe in a God who seems to have forgotten us. Darkness is part of the school for the soul, an opportunity to delve into what really matters. It causes us to put away all that is frivolous or vain and to sift through our lives to find the treasures. When we are desperate, we are serious, focused on what life is all about, and what He is all about.

His Promises

Many sorrows come to the wicked,
but unfailing love surrounds those who trust the LORD.

PSALM 32:10

But when I am afraid,
I will put my trust in you.
I praise God for what he has promised.
I trust in God, so why should I be afraid?
What can mere mortals do to me?

PSALM 56:3-4

If you make the LORD your refuge,
if you make the Most High your shelter,
no evil will conquer you;
no plague will come near your home.
For he will order his angels
to protect you wherever you go.

PSALM 91:9-11

A THOUSAND LITTLE MOMENTS

As mothers, our days are made up of thousands of little moments, insignificant to the public eye: changing one more diaper, listening to the heart's cry of one more teenager, encouraging our spouses through one more year of financial difficulty, living through one more season of faith when it all has felt overwhelming.

Isolation and loneliness are aching companions at different times—feeling that we don't fit in with many people—feeling lost in the storms of life.

Other times, we feel as though we might drown from the weight of our children's lives: trying to keep them afloat; struggling with differing personalities; meeting their needs, answering their spiritual demands; and bearing with them through very difficult seasons like the sleepless nights of babyhood and the mysterious years of toddlerhood, all the trials and joys of elementary school, teenage storms, and young adult decisions and pressures.

Yet somewhere, deep inside, God gave us a tenaciousness to keep going through the storms, to keep trusting Him, to keep believing Him, to have faith that He is good, even when we don't feel His presence.

Integrity in these seemingly insignificant moments will become the measure of integrity over a lifetime and build a picture of faithfulness for others to recall when they go through their own hard times: "Oh, I remember—Mom kept going. She kept loving. She kept believing. I guess I can too. Her story is my foundation for encouragement."

Keep going. Keep loving. Keep believing. You can—because He does.

His Promises

So be strong and courageous! Do not be afraid and do not panic before them. For the LORD your God will personally go ahead of you. He will neither fail you nor abandon you.

DEUTERONOMY 31:6

He heals the brokenhearted
  and bandages their wounds.

PSALM 147:3

Three different times I begged the Lord to take it away. Each time he said, "My grace is all you need. My power works best in weakness." So now I am glad to boast about my weaknesses, so that the power of Christ can work through me. That's why I take pleasure in my weaknesses, and in the insults, hardships, persecutions, and troubles that I suffer for Christ. For when I am weak, then I am strong.

2 CORINTHIANS 12:8-10

LET IT GO!

Women can be so uptight and prone to worry, can't we? Each of us has been given a different puzzle— different circumstances, gifts, personalities, families, children, husbands (or lack thereof). I wish I had not been such a people pleaser, trying to live up to the expectations of others—my family, my critics, my peers. My family puzzle just did not fit into the pattern of others' expectations, so trying to live up to those standards was impossible. I wish I had accepted that at the very first instead of fretting about things I could not change.

Some of the cards we have been dealt are pleasing, and some just drive us crazy. But I think the reason we often struggle with His will is because we find ourselves and our circumstances unacceptable, embarrassing, and/or less than perfect.

We can't truly find peace until we relinquish a tight grasp on our rights and learn to rest in the places in which we find ourselves.

To have peace and rest, we must die to ourselves, our failures, and our expectations and hold our hands up to our Father just as a toddler would and say, "I need You. I need Your love, grace, joy, peace today. Without You, I am not able to experience rest in my heart. Help me to see Your presence in this place, this time, these circumstances, within my own limitations. Open my eyes to beauty, to Your fingerprints all around me today."

His Promises

Come to me, all of you who are weary and carry heavy burdens, and I will give you rest. Take my yoke upon you. Let me teach you, because I am humble and gentle at heart, and you will find rest for your souls. For my yoke is easy to bear, and the burden I give you is light.

MATTHEW 11:28-30

Don't let your hearts be troubled. Trust in God, and trust also in me.

JOHN 14:1

The LORD is a shelter for the oppressed,
*   a refuge in times of trouble.*
*   Those who know your name trust in you,*
*   for you, O LORD, do not abandon those who*
*   search for you.*

PSALM 9:9-10

FORGET
THE RULES

God is such a wonderful provider for us. Take a moment to look at nature and all the flowers and color and creatures that He crafted for our pleasure. When sin separated us from Him, He came among us, giving up the comfort, glory, and honor He held in heaven to serve, feed, live with, and encourage His own precious disciples.

Our life with God is not just made up of a list of rules He has given us. He comes as the servant King, the One who lays down His life, the One who is humble and meek. God gives us wisdom and guidance so that our lives will be healthy, strong, and protected.

This becomes our pattern for parenting. He served and loved and sacrificed and gave of Himself so that we would long to be holy out of our gratitude, reverence, and love for Him. He called His disciples to serve, to love, and to be holy. He gave them true life and beauty that filled their deepest needs, as well as fulfilling their longings to live a purposeful life.

Getting the rules right and defining theology correctly will not make our children want to serve God. It is laying down our lives for them—serving them, listening to them, loving who God made them to be, that will give them a desire to love God with all their hearts. By experiencing our love for them, they will more easily understand and receive God's love, as it will already be familiar to their hearts and minds.

His Promises

God saved you by his grace when you believed. And you can't take credit for this; it is a gift from God. Salvation is not a reward for the good things we have done, so none of us can boast about it.

EPHESIANS 2:8-9

They replied, "We want to perform God's works, too. What should we do?" Jesus told them, "This is the only work God wants from you: Believe in the one he has sent."

JOHN 6:28-29

Yet we know that a person is made right with God by faith in Jesus Christ, not by obeying the law. And we have believed in Christ Jesus, so that we might be made right with God because of our faith in Christ, not because we have obeyed the law. For no one will ever be made right with God by obeying the law.

GALATIANS 2:16

CLIMBING
THE WALLS

All of us have walls in our lives—circumstances that seem to stop our forward motion. If only we had more money, help, friends; if only we weren't plagued by this illness or difficult marriage, or, or, or . . .

The glory of a woman who has Christ in her life is to mount those walls. If we believe in Him, we have no other choice than to live by what we know to be true, regardless of our feelings, the circumstances, our friends' thoughts, or the world's opinion of our circumstances. It is to God's glory for us to live supernaturally.

Our heart is unable to speak into other people's lives unless we have personal experience mounting some of the same walls they're being faced with. Overcoming gives us a greater capacity for faith, compassion, and understanding of others in this battle of life.

David faced so many incredibly difficult, seemingly insurmountable walls yet embraced God and believed that He was good. Because of this God-focused heart, he was chosen by God to have an inheritance forever and was called a man after God's heart.

And so, it is to the honor of a godly woman, in the presence of her family and friends, to mount the walls in her life with joy that comes from obedience, with strength that comes from trusting God, and with beauty that comes from choosing to believe in God's goodness and light in the midst of darkness.

His Promises

Be happy with those who are happy, and weep with those who weep.

ROMANS 12:15

Since God chose you to be the holy people he loves, you must clothe yourselves with tenderhearted mercy, kindness, humility, gentleness, and patience.

COLOSSIANS 3:12

When I am with those who are weak, I share their weakness, for I want to bring the weak to Christ. Yes, I try to find common ground with everyone, doing everything I can to save some.

1 CORINTHIANS 9:22

COMING UP SHORT

It is simple to see all the flaws in our children and ourselves. And it would be easy for us to take the blame for our children's failures, since we are their mother and responsible for training them! However, rather than focusing on the bad, it's more beneficial to focus on faith and the potential someday to be realized after years of praying and seeing God work. It's better to have faith that God can take my honest offering of steadfastness and hope.

He will make up for our deficits. Though we don't understand why bad things happen, He is stronger and bigger than all the "bad," and in His time, He will redeem it all. Faith must be in His power and not our own. Rather than focusing on our own lack of strength, we trust His ability to reach our children. Giving Him our best, we leave the results in His hands, waiting for His timing. This relinquishing happens one minute at a time—one detail at a time.

When the enemy convinces us that our concentration should be placed on what is lacking in our lives, our personality flaws, our family's difficult places, we become unable to affect the world in a positive way. And that is a terrible loss indeed.

His Promises

I—yes, I alone—will blot out your sins for my own sake and will never think of them again.

ISAIAH 43:25

Imitate God, therefore, in everything you do, because you are his dear children. Live a life filled with love, following the example of Christ. He loved us and offered himself as a sacrifice for us, a pleasing aroma to God.

EPHESIANS 5:1-2

He is so rich in kindness and grace that he purchased our freedom with the blood of his Son and forgave our sins.

EPHESIANS 1:7

WEATHERING
THE STORM

Storms of culture and life are common, and they wreak havoc with us as we are tossed about from without and within. As we look at the wild waves threatening to overcome us, panic is a natural response. Fear paralyzes.

There are three things we can do in the midst of those storms to counteract this:

1. **Remember and list all of the ways you have seen God's faithfulness and answers to prayer.** Even in the most difficult years, you can look back and see His handprints in your life—always there, always providing.
2. **Find a promise, and hold fast to His Word.** Have you ever been in the car with your children and all of them start speaking to you at once, as though you can hear their voices above the roar? The voices of the world, fear of what-ifs, all speaking at once, drown out His voice. We must still our lives and sit quietly, that He may speak to us.

3. **Determine to hold fast and to be a courageous warrior in your battles.** Your children are looking to your story to give them courage in the stories they will yet live. Hold fast, find a friend to pray with, and stand strong. You only have the promise of this moment to proclaim His faithfulness in your own life for all generations to see.

His Promises

Never let loyalty and kindness leave you!
Tie them around your neck as a reminder.
    Write them deep within your heart.
Then you will find favor with both God and people,
    and you will earn a good reputation.

PROVERBS 3:3-4

He gives power to the weak
    and strength to the powerless.
Even youths will become weak and tired,
    and young men will fall in exhaustion.
But those who trust in the Lord will find new strength.
    They will soar high on wings like eagles.
They will run and not grow weary.
    They will walk and not faint.

ISAIAH 40:29-31

If you need wisdom, ask our generous God, and he will give it to you. He will not rebuke you for asking.

JAMES 1:5

WELCOME TO YOUR STORY

Who doesn't love a rousing tale of heroes saving damsels in distress, romantic accounts of valor and sacrifice in history, or heartwarming tales of family, home, and children?

Scripture is full of dramatic stories of bravery (David and Goliath), romance (Ruth and Boaz), courage (Moses stepping into the Red Sea with a couple million children, animals, and adults screaming behind him, being chased by the strongest army ever known), and so many more. And of course, each of us is also living a story.

Maybe yours doesn't feel exciting at this moment or strategic in light of history. But most people who are considered heroes of the faith were normal people amid normal life circumstances who trusted God even when the others surrounding them were naysayers and could not see Him.

The story told about you in the future depends on the story you are living today.

In other words, the situation you find yourself in today, whether it requires excellence in morality, courageous endurance, faithful belief, or overcoming love, is the basis of your integrity or lack of integrity tomorrow. You cannot leave a story of faithfulness in the minds and hearts of your children, grandchildren, and others unless you actually live your story with faith, courage, moral excellence, self-discipline, and sacrificial love today.

His Promises

Overwhelming victory is ours through Christ, who loved us.
ROMANS 8:37

God blesses those who are humble,
for they will inherit the whole earth.
God blesses those who hunger and thirst for justice,
for they will be satisfied.
God blesses those who are merciful,
for they will be shown mercy.
God blesses those whose hearts are pure,
for they will see God.
God blesses those who work for peace,
for they will be called the children of God.
MATTHEW 5:5-9

For every child of God defeats this evil world, and we achieve this victory through our faith.
1 JOHN 5:4

WORTH EVERY PENNY

The problem with knowing we as mothers are called to build a heritage of godly leaders right in our own homes is that most of us have had no training, preparation, or education to prepare us for what it would take or how much it would cost! Most of us just got married with the hope that someone would love and take care of us, providing security and affirmation, and then babies came and overwhelmed us. We had never been trained for this job, had perhaps not seen it modeled well as we grew up, and were never given a vision for how powerful a family that stood for God could be, or how much work it would take to build.

So, overwhelmed women who have never had the opportunity to build a plan for this vision may find themselves up to their eyeballs in details and duties and caring for babies without sufficient support, input, accountability, or help from experienced women who have built godly legacies. This is the greatest job in the world, one that will indeed influence what our nation becomes. It's worth investing time and effort to help prepare these precious and significant moms for how to do it.

Satan would love nothing more than for us to continue minimizing the importance of deeply investing our time and lives into the minds, hearts, souls, and training of our children, because he knows they are essential to bringing the Kingdom of God to bear in their generation.

His Promises

Humanly speaking, it is impossible. But with God everything is possible.

MATTHEW 19:26

Think about the things of heaven, not the things of earth.

COLOSSIANS 3:2

Give your burdens to the LORD,
and he will take care of you.
He will not permit the godly to slip and fall.

PSALM 55:22

DO YOU
READ ME?

One of the greatest ways we can love our children is by cultivating in them a love for learning, growing their intellect and giving them a broad base of education.

There is nothing more helpful for building the soul or drawing children to your ideas of faith than investing long hours reading together. A child does not just turn into a reader by chance; it is a cultivated habit, a discipline of life.

If you really want to give your children this profound gift of love, you must stop the other things you are doing and read every day. If you wait until you have time, it will never happen.

Delight in great stories, and teach the written word passionately. Treasure words and ideas and history in front of your children so that they will fall in love with language.

Plan a great list of wonderful books to cozy up and read with your children. Make it a daily ritual. Cuddle up on the couch. Use great voices. Get excited!

If we lose the gift of reading in this generation, we will lose the ability to reason, to understand God's greatness, to think well, to have convictions. We must keep literacy up! It is one of the most important works of our lives. If children do not learn to love to read, they will not become readers of the Bible—the best words. They will love reading if you read out loud to them and cherish them and celebrate great stories together with them in peace and joy.

His Promises

Intelligent people are always ready to learn.
Their ears are open for knowledge.

PROVERBS 18:15

Instruct the wise,
and they will be even wiser.
Teach the righteous,
and they will learn even more.

PROVERBS 9:9

Show me the right path, O LORD;
point out the road for me to follow.

PSALM 25:4

THE POWER
OF LOVE

Our feelings are a gift from God. Our feelings of love, compassion, mercy, sympathy, and tenderness are a part of our glory as women. When we exercise our feelings of love toward those whom God has brought into our lives—our friends, children, husbands, acquaintances—we bring great encouragement and strength to them.

But as deeply emotional beings, we are also very susceptible to feelings of guilt, inadequacy, fear, and insecurity. These negative feelings can grip us and build a stronghold in our hearts. They can keep us captive to the dark voices we often hear, either from others who have wrongly influenced our lives or from our own feelings of failure.

Loving generously and deeply is a beautiful mantle for a woman to wear. Jesus said that Christians would be truly known in the world by our love—unconditional, redeeming love for one another.

We must understand that Satan, the archenemy of God, knows how very powerful the love of Christ through us can be. He would do almost anything to keep us from understanding our great value to God. He whispers to us that we are not worthy in hopes that he can keep us from living a story worth telling through the days of our lives!

We cannot be free to love as long as we are dwelling on ourselves—our own inadequacies, bitterness, or lack of forgiveness for ourselves or for others.

His Promises

Don't just pretend to love others. Really love them. Hate what is wrong. Hold tightly to what is good.

ROMANS 12:9

Owe nothing to anyone—except for your obligation to love one another. If you love your neighbor, you will fulfill the requirements of God's law.

ROMANS 13:8

But God showed his great love for us by sending Christ to die for us while we were still sinners.

ROMANS 5:8

PRIORITY
ONE

It seems to have become a cultural value to be busy and justify ourselves by our activities. We seem to forget that God is our Father and that a good Father would not expect His little child to carry the load. Sometimes, when we have a lot on our plate, the best thing we can do is reassess and cut back, so we can focus only on the agenda He has set.

Christ needs to be at our center. We need to have peace and quiet in our soul. We can say *no*, no matter how many people there are who seem to need us, so we can live at peace.

We are a baby to God, His toddler. He is in control. He does not want to abuse us. He does not want us to be neurotic and angry. He wants us to be at peace—sleeping in the boat in the midst of the storm, because we are resting in His ability to take care of things.

There will always be opportunities, but now is a good time to pace yourself, to still your soul, to seek to live more simply, to say yes to your God-given priorities and no to all that will take you away. Yes, you could do lots more, but then you would become crazy and grumpy and tight and hard to live with, living by your own flesh and striving and works—and you cannot hold His hand and behave in such a manner all at the same time.

His Promises

The LORD himself will fight for you. Just stay calm.
EXODUS 14:14

Open my eyes to see
the wonderful truths in your instructions.
PSALM 119:18

Be still in the presence of the LORD,
and wait patiently for him to act.
PSALM 37:7

BROKEN
RECORD

We are all broken, and this world we live in is a broken place, where death of heart, of relationships, of love is prevalent. Often we mask deep, dark feelings of regret over various failures: Failure with our children—having shown anger or neglect to them, not really liking them, or doing everything we could to reach their hearts but ending up with a prodigal who breaks our heart. Failure with friends—petty quarrels, difficulty forgiving and forgetting. Living with habits such as eating disorders, overspending, cherishing idols we know consume our souls, reading dark novels, or more darkness with sexual habits than we can admit.

We are all broken people. Yet, we must understand that He does not define us by our failures. He is "mindful that we are but dust" (Psalm 103:14, NASB). It is an illusion that anyone you know is perfect or can become perfect through lots of effort. No one can. All we like sheep have gone astray. We simply cannot hold to our ideals by striving toward them, and we are all in total need of His mercy and grace every day.

We want to serve Him. We want to be holy. We intend to be gracious, loving, and patient. But we all fail and fall short, again and again and again.

So, do not judge others—or yourself! But love outrageously, deeply, compassionately, just as He, gentle in spirit, has you. And in consequence, we will see love—deep, grateful, healing love—abounding, flowing out all over, because of Him.

His Promises

So now there is no condemnation for those who belong to Christ Jesus.

ROMANS 8:1

Three different times I begged the Lord to take it away. Each time he said, "My grace is all you need. My power works best in weakness." So now I am glad to boast about my weaknesses, so that the power of Christ can work through me. That's why I take pleasure in my weaknesses, and in the insults, hardships, persecutions, and troubles that I suffer for Christ. For when I am weak, then I am strong.

2 CORINTHIANS 12:8-10

Judge not, and you will not be judged; condemn not, and you will not be condemned; forgive, and you will be forgiven.

LUKE 6:37, ESV

UNSUNG HEROES

Most of "mama life" is invisible. This noble cause we embrace is often fraught with relentless repetition, exhaustion, draining of our emotions, and spiritual challenges. Yet it is also the very place we are called to worship. This is the place faith is being forged and character is being modeled and love is going deep into the hearts and minds of our children. What you are doing matters so much! And Jesus, who sacrificed His time, His emotions, and ultimately His very body, sees you and is so very pleased, cheering you on from the heavenly realm.

No one says to you, "Yay! You chose to be patient with one more ear infection and sleepless night!" Or "Congratulations! You are the queen of children with health challenges and learning issues!" Or "Wow! You are so very patient with those hormonal teenagers." Or "You just waited for your toddler to get over his tantrum, and you handled it patiently. You are a hero!"

As mothers, our homes and all the little choices of each day become our sanctuary of worship, our sacrifice of praise. Bringing light into the potentially dark corners of our lives together, singing and dancing and celebrating God's reality in the mundaneness of dishes, late nights of Winnie-the-Pooh and ear infections and steamy showers to alleviate croup—these are the places our children feel the comfort and grace of His touch through you. And that matters more than you can imagine.

His Promises

Don't be selfish; don't try to impress others. Be humble, thinking of others as better than yourselves.

PHILIPPIANS 2:3

He leads the humble in doing right,
teaching them his way.

PSALM 25:9

For God is working in you, giving you the desire and the power to do what pleases him.

PHILIPPIANS 2:13

FOLLOW
THE LIGHT!

When the life of Jesus is in our midst, there is a palpable crackle in the air, a sparkle to the lights and shadows of His dance among us.

Yet most people I know, including me so much of the time, live as though their feet are tied to the ground by heavy loads of duty, works, guilt, worry, comparison, inadequacy, boredom . . . etc., etc., etc. He did not create us to live in such a way. He came to give life, and life more abundant. The joy of the Lord is to be our strength. What have the voices of this world done to our joy?

Who in your life points you passionately, irresistibly into the arms of a loving God, a gentle Shepherd, a compassionate Father, an interesting Artist? He is the God who longs for us to celebrate life, to exist above the mundane present to perceive the invisible life of the Kingdom He is shaping through us for eternity.

Knowing Him should create in us a powerful sense

of life, excellence, expectancy from a heart filled with faith, love, and anticipation.

Jesus "was the true Light which, coming into the world, enlightens every man" (John 1:9, NASB). In leaving everything behind and pursuing Him—not rules or laws or formula or morality, but the Person who has so much more to offer—we find light and life. His Kingdom is the pearl of great price, worth selling all that we have in order to grasp it and hold it fast.

His Promises

And this is the way to have eternal life—to know you, the only true God, and Jesus Christ, the one you sent to earth.
JOHN 17:3

I love those who love me,
and those who seek me diligently find me.
PROVERBS 8:17, ESV

Take delight in the LORD,
and he will give you your heart's desires.
PSALM 37:4

MOMENTARY MIRACLES

Jesus is in the world today, at this moment.

He is present and alive, His Spirit blowing through the moments of our days. He is seeking someone to heal, someone to save, someone to whom He can extend redeeming love—and it will all happen through mere humans, those whose feet are made of clay. He is alive, and He lives through us.

All of us, with different skills, shapes, personalities, liabilities, and stories, are here for a short few years to faithfully live out a miracle. His presence invades the things of the earth. His love permeates the places of the lonely, His joy fills the air—but how? Through *us*. He is in us and wants to bring the miracle of Himself to this world, through limited, earthly jars of clay.

How will we honor this vast miracle of His life in us?

Today, who needs us to give something He wants to provide?

What do we have in us today that His Spirit would give to those present in our lives?

Someone needs His words of encouragement and hope—who is the person He would love through us?

Someone needs a cup of cold water, a sandwich, a cup of tea, an eye-to-eye encounter that says, "You are of great value—you are not condemned. I love you. He loves you." Who will that be?

His Promises

Don't store up treasures here on earth, where moths eat them and rust destroys them, and where thieves break in and steal. Store your treasures in heaven, where moths and rust cannot destroy, and thieves do not break in and steal. Wherever your treasure is, there the desires of your heart will also be.

MATTHEW 6:19-21

Don't do your good deeds publicly, to be admired by others, for you will lose the reward from your Father in heaven. When you give to someone in need, don't do as the hypocrites do—blowing trumpets in the synagogues and streets to call attention to their acts of charity! I tell you the truth, they have received all the reward they will ever get. But when you give to someone in need, don't let your left hand know what your right hand is doing. Give your gifts in private, and your Father, who sees everything, will reward you.

MATTHEW 6:1-4

For I was hungry, and you fed me. I was thirsty, and you gave me a drink. I was a stranger, and you invited me into your home.

MATTHEW 25:35

LOVE BEYOND REASON

Raising a family can be fraught with weariness, frustration, darkness, hurt feelings, criticism, difficult children, stress in marriage—you name it. Anyone who would take on this enormous task of subduing and civilizing your home, your family, and your lives in a culture and time in which families are being torn apart and children's souls are being filled with darkness and despair is a true hero!

God wants us to understand that when we prevail over darkness in the power of His Spirit, through faith and obedience, we live out the reality of His power and presence in the same way that Jesus did when He was alive on earth.

There is no rational reason why someone would give up her life, her body, her time, her rights, for the well-being and building up of someone else. Servant mothers throughout history have portrayed Christ by living sacrificially and giving up their lives for others.

So today I wish you courage as you overcome. May you have a sense of victory and affirmation that you are among those who are modeling the reality of His great heart and soul by each tiny act of faith, as you choose to love the little ones in your home, when you choose to serve by making your home a lighthouse of righteousness, and when you bring the grace of forgiveness and peace to those who have fallen short.

His Promises

Patient endurance is what you need now, so that you will continue to do God's will. Then you will receive all that he has promised.

HEBREWS 10:36

Let us run with endurance the race God has set before us. We do this by keeping our eyes on Jesus, the champion who initiates and perfects our faith.

HEBREWS 12:1-2

When your faith is tested, your endurance has a chance to grow. So let it grow, for when your endurance is fully developed, you will be perfect and complete, needing nothing.

JAMES 1:3-4

FIND YOUR
FOCUS

We live in a world that values the opinions of others very highly. Seeking to keep up with the Joneses is an age-old pursuit. But Scripture is clear: God wants our focus to be on Him.

In a world that gives us permission to be self-centered, we constantly look at ourselves and our pictures on social media, listening for the notification that says someone has "liked" us. We become our own idols, striving for recognition and affirmation. It is not wrong to desire to be loved and to belong, but Jesus meant for us to find our meaning first in Him, then in our family, our community of believers, and those we serve in our own day-to-day lives.

In the story of the Good Samaritan, Jesus tells of those who could publicly pontificate and argue the law and posture on their supposed righteousness, yet these men neglected those who really needed redemption and help, embodied by the man caught by robbers, left for dead beside the road.

When we live in true integrity, following hard after Him, our children can find the real Jesus living in our home. Not someone who wants to keep up appearances, but the real Christ who lays down His life and shepherds the sheep of His fold, the servant King who cares about the unseen people.

True personal integrity comes from following hard after Him and loving those He has called us to love and doing what He has called us to do.

His Promises

And what do you benefit if you gain the whole world but are yourself lost or destroyed?

LUKE 9:25

Obviously, I'm not trying to win the approval of people, but of God. If pleasing people were my goal, I would not be Christ's servant.

GALATIANS 1:10

We are careful to be honorable before the Lord, but we also want everyone else to see that we are honorable.

2 CORINTHIANS 8:21

TRUTH AND CONSEQUENCES

We live in a culture that tries to convince us that we can do it all. However, each of us only has one life to invest in what matters. Each of us is limited in the amount of time we can use to invest in the priorities of our lives. We have to choose what we will focus on—and our choices will have lasting consequences.

Pouring into the souls of our children, developing sharp minds, protecting them from the draw of culture, passing on faith—these do not come about by chance. God will hold us responsible for the ways we use our lives to cultivate the spiritual lives of our children.

Our hearts must be devoted to the stewardship of the young lives that have been entrusted into our hands. We cannot serve the world and God's purposes.

He allows us free rein, the ability to ignore and go against biblical logic and wisdom, but we will usually be left to live with the consequences of unwise choices.

If children do not find stability, love, training, spiritual reality, purpose, and comfort in their own homes, they will look for them wherever they can find them. They will become like the places where they spend the most time and like the people they spend the most time with, because they are shaped by the culture in which they invest their hearts.

His Promises

Commit your actions to the LORD,
and your plans will succeed.

PROVERBS 16:3

Not that I have already obtained this or am already
perfect, but I press on to make it my own, because Christ
Jesus has made me his own. Brothers, I do not consider
that I have made it my own. But one thing I do: forgetting
what lies behind and straining forward to what lies ahead,
I press on toward the goal for the prize of the upward call
of God in Christ Jesus.

PHILIPPIANS 3:12-14, ESV

Look straight ahead,
and fix your eyes on what lies before you.

PROVERBS 4:25

LONG-RANGE VISION

A "yes" to time watching somersaults in the backyard is a "no" to a phone call, a glance through a magazine, or a bit of alone time. A "yes" to asking friends over for a time of encouragement is a "no" to the free time you might have spent on yourself. "Yes" to the car pool means "no" to sleeping in; "yes" to playing during bath time means "no" to your favorite television show . . . and on it goes.

As moms, what we really need is long-range vision! While the decision to draw your circle of direct influence a little smaller might appear to minimize who you are, the truth lies elsewhere. Think about a drop of food coloring splashed into a cup of water. The more water, the more diluted the color. And so it is with each one of us. When we spread ourselves thin, leaving no time for snuggles and back rubs, Bible study and reading deeply, family vacations and Saturday afternoons at the park, our influence becomes diluted.

So, may I suggest something, mama? Feel free to say lots of "yeses" to your littles, and lots of "nos" to others. Limit yourself in this season of mothering young ones, and watch your influence grow where it's most important.

I have never heard a woman say, "I wish I would have worked more hours while my children were young" or "I wish I would have read more magazines and watched fewer somersaults." Rather, the longing is for time long slipped away.

His Promises

We can make our plans,
but the LORD determines our steps.
PROVERBS 16:9

For everything there is a season,
a time for every activity under heaven.
ECCLESIASTES 3:1

But generous people plan to do what is generous,
and they stand firm in their generosity.
ISAIAH 32:8

DON'T BE AFRAID
OF THE DARK

Darkness invades our lives more often than we would like or expect. When news of another tragedy explodes over social media or the news, we feel sorrowful and angry, and sometimes afraid and confused. Our children, of course, experience all this too.

While we tend to our own spirits in such difficult times, we mamas must remember we also tenderly hold the hearts of our own children. We need to be guardians of the flame of faith inside of them, until they are old enough to guard their hearts themselves. In a world of media and video games and TV and movies and cell phones that can carry the images of all sorts of evil, one of the best gifts we can give to our children is the gift of an innocent, protected heart.

Children are made to be innocent, to believe in mystery, to be good and pure of heart. The longer we can keep them in this place of storing up hope, and believing in miracles, the better. So, when a tragedy occurs, we must, as the strong ones, bear up the difficulty and tragedy inside our own hearts, pray, and walk with the Lord and in the comfort of other spiritually mature adults.

We must seek Him who is the light in the darkness and look more profoundly into Scripture, which reminds us that we, and our world, indeed need a Savior. He is with us, He is our hope, and He has never, ever left us alone.

His Promises

Jesus said, "Let the children come to me. Don't stop them! For the Kingdom of Heaven belongs to those who are like these children."

MATTHEW 19:14

Whoever causes one of these little ones who believe in me to sin, it would be better for him to have a great millstone fastened around his neck and to be drowned in the depth of the sea.

MATTHEW 18:6, ESV

Anyone who welcomes a little child like this on my behalf welcomes me, and anyone who welcomes me welcomes not only me but also my Father who sent me.

MARK 9:37

MORE VALUABLE
THAN GOLD

It is not the grand, noble accomplishments that are most profoundly valuable to God, but the unnoticed, invisible moments of being faithful and courageous when no one else is looking that become the jewels of our faith in the eyes of God.

Accepting a loud, boisterous child and seeking to be patient and gentle over and over again when feelings threaten to erupt into frustration and anger. Working beyond exhaustion and getting up in the middle of the night, again, for a sick child. Enduring the heavy burdens and tests of marriage. Cleaning up messes again and again and again. Making one more homemade meal and drawing the family circle together to celebrate life when a nap seemed more desirable. Having one more devotional in the midst of wiggly, distracted children, and believing that somehow eternity is entering their hearts.

These and more are the noble and valiant works

of motherhood. While we may worry the instability of our family life would ruin our children, or that our own personal flaws would harm them, the Holy Spirit is making them strong, showing them how to exercise muscles of faith in dark situations.

His Promises

But the Holy Spirit produces this kind of fruit in our lives: love, joy, peace, patience, kindness, goodness, faithfulness.

GALATIANS 5:22

Now if you will obey me and keep my covenant, you will be my own special treasure from among all the peoples on earth.

EXODUS 19:5

Be filled with the Spirit, addressing one another in psalms and hymns and spiritual songs, singing and making melody to the Lord with your heart, giving thanks always and for everything to God the Father in the name of our Lord Jesus Christ, submitting to one another out of reverence for Christ.

EPHESIANS 5:18-21, ESV

GIVING 110%

Scripture tells us to "train up a child in the way he should go" (Proverbs 22:6, NASB). For this reason, training is essential to the well-being of a child, so he or she may live life in a strong and healthy way.

Training can be illustrated in many ways: an athlete must learn and train to become a champion. A pianist must be instructed and practice to become a concert performer. An artist must learn the skills and philosophy of drawing and painting and then practice to become masterful at his or her craft. And so it is with any craft or skill.

Shouldn't all true believers be able to call forth excellence and integrity as a reflection of Him in our lives? Yet excellence and integrity are personal issues. One can only grow in these areas through personal commitment and a decision that says, "Regardless of what is happening around me, I will be the best I can be, work the hardest I am able, and pursue the highest standards, especially for my personal life where no one but God sees. My worship of God requires that I pursue the standard of His holiness as an affirmation of His reality in my life."

This labor of excellence, personally and in the lives of our children, will take many long years. But if we are not committed to pursuing whatever it takes to build this excellence, then what hope do we have for our future, and how can we represent Him, who has given all?

His Promises

Praise the LORD, who is my rock.
He trains my hands for war
    and gives my fingers skill for battle.

PSALM 144:1

Do not waste time arguing over godless ideas and old wives' tales. Instead, train yourself to be godly. Physical training is good, but training for godliness is much better, promising benefits in this life and in the life to come.

1 TIMOTHY 4:7-8

Athletes cannot win the prize unless they follow the rules.

2 TIMOTHY 2:5

R-E-S-P-E-C-T

When we read biblical accounts of people who saw the glory of God, they are often bowing down in reverence and hiding their eyes because it is so wonderful and great. Yet that response is far removed from our experience today. All that used to be considered sacred, whether people, places, even concepts like marriage and childhood, are regularly devalued and ridiculed in contemporary culture.

We must give our children not just knowledge of what the word *holy* means but tangible practices where they can come to understand that some things are sacred and set apart, deserving of our reverence and worship.

Consequently, as we begin the training of our little children's hearts and souls, we must figure out how to convey to them that life is not about us but about pleasing, serving, loving, worshiping, and living for the very One who is the Lord of the universe, the Creator of the world, and the King forever.

One way to implement a sense of reverence and holiness in the lives of our children is teaching them that there are places to use "quiet voices and respectful hearts"—like in church, at concerts, at funerals, at graduations, at recitals. Before you go into these places, talk to your children about your expectations ahead of time.

If this is not built into your children's daily life, when it comes to adulthood, there will be no pattern, no practiced understanding of what it means to love and obey our Lord with wholehearted devotion.

His Promises

Since we are receiving a Kingdom that is unshakable, let us be thankful and please God by worshiping him with holy fear and awe.

HEBREWS 12:28

You must keep my Sabbath days of rest and show reverence for my sanctuary. I am the LORD.

LEVITICUS 26:2

Fear of the LORD is the foundation of wisdom.
Knowledge of the Holy One results in good judgment.

PROVERBS 9:10

STEP BY STEP

When your children walk with you, are they walking with a wise person? Can they look at your seasoned responses, your insightful understanding of people, your fortitude in difficult times as they walk with you in the moments of your daily life? If you think about it, teaching our children to walk never really ends. They watch us, listen to us when we speak to others, hear us talking with our husband behind closed doors. Our lives are the walk that our children will imitate.

With confusing voices, compromised ideals, wavering morals, secular values, and so many opposing opinions, where will our children find clarity and strong, secure values to embrace? As mothers, we must be ready and equipped with steady feet and strong souls to lead the way for our children with integrity. We will give them confidence as we walk, staying close to them, holding their hands, and showing them sure footsteps to follow.

No matter how old your children become, you are the example for them. They will always be looking at you for a vision of integrity, ideals, and ways to interact with God. The longer you provide your children with wisdom based on truth, the more they will consider your advice as they walk their own adult journey.

His Promises

Direct your children onto the right path,
and when they are older, they will not leave it.

PROVERBS 22:6

The LORD is our God, the LORD alone. And you must love the LORD your God with all your heart, all your soul, and all your strength. And you must commit yourselves wholeheartedly to these commands that I am giving you today. Repeat them again and again to your children. Talk about them when you are at home and when you are on the road, when you are going to bed and when you are getting up.

DEUTERONOMY 6:4-7

"For the LORD disciplines those he loves, and he punishes each one he accepts as his child." As you endure this divine discipline, remember that God is treating you as his own children.

HEBREWS 12:6-7

GIVE ME
A BREAK

Contrary to all the commercials promoting products made to help you keep going despite your cold, your exhaustion, or your depression, the truth is that God understands that life can, at times, be overwhelming, and He actually wants us to take a break from all the activity happening around us. In fact, the Hebrews were given a law about setting aside one day a week for rest; they were forbidden to do work of any kind. Jesus taught that the law had been made for man, so that we might experience rest.

I think sometimes we stay busy because we are insecure. The voices in our heads tell us we are supposed to do all that our friends are doing, even if it leaves us in a frenzy. We have developed the idea that if we stop, if we don't meet the needs of everyone around us, every second of the day, if we don't answer the phone, if we don't take that position at church, if we don't go to this event, and if we don't answer that e-mail, the world will stop on its axis, and somehow, we will be disappointing God. But His Word tells us something different.

His Promises

Then Jesus said, "Come to me, all of you who are weary and carry heavy burdens, and I will give you rest. Take my yoke upon you. Let me teach you, because I am humble and gentle at heart, and you will find rest for your souls."

MATTHEW 11:28-29

For I have given rest to the weary and joy to the sorrowing.

JEREMIAH 31:25

So there is a special rest still waiting for the people of God. For all who have entered into God's rest have rested from their labors, just as God did after creating the world. So let us do our best to enter that rest.

HEBREWS 4:9-11

TUG OF WAR

Motherhood is a never-ending sacrifice of your time, effort, body: yourself. You are working uphill against sinful little creatures who do not like it when you push against their little selfish wills, so they have various ways of pushing back.

During the toddler years, they fall on the floor and throw a fit because you didn't let them eat the candy they wanted. In the teen years, they question your wisdom and integrity and know just where to put in the knife. After all, none of us have been perfect, and we all have flaws, and our children tend to discover most of them.

Then there are always Job's friends in the crowd—those people who are quite sure they know why your life is not going well and what you have done wrong to make your life such a mess. Yet Job's friends were quite wrong! Job was being persecuted by Satan because Satan thought if a person was persecuted, he could not remain loyal to God. God had actually chosen

Job as a model of integrity and faith, and Job's friends could not have been more wrong in their statements about his demise.

So don't pay attention to the critics. Their voices, though sometimes strong, are just part of journeying through this path of parenting and life. Let us seek instead to accept our limitations, refuel, keep going, focus on pleasing the One who is always going to be on our team—our heavenly Father, whose voice is always there to encourage.

His Promises

I pray that God, the source of hope, will fill you completely with joy and peace because you trust in him. Then you will overflow with confident hope through the power of the Holy Spirit.

ROMANS 15:13

Don't copy the behavior and customs of this world, but let God transform you into a new person by changing the way you think. Then you will learn to know God's will for you, which is good and pleasing and perfect.

ROMANS 12:2

For we speak as messengers approved by God to be entrusted with the Good News. Our purpose is to please God, not people. He alone examines the motives of our hearts.

1 THESSALONIANS 2:4

HOW THE COOKIE CUTTER CRUMBLES

There are so many possibilities when it comes to the various personalities and tendencies we may encounter in our children. Extroverts need to talk more and have lots of activities and people in their lives; introverts need more time alone to ponder, create, and go into their inner sanctum to be refreshed.

Some children just really want affirmation and hugs and listening so they will *feel* loved. Others want you to do something with them—to be active alongside you. Others want sympathy and to have you understand all that's on their hearts. Still others thrive on quality time.

We are to accept and cooperate with our children's God-given personalities because God has work for them to do in this world that matches their personality and gifting. If we want to be God's instrument to open their hearts, we have to study who they are and reach each one according to the personal design of his or her heart.

Children are not cookie-cutter copies of each other who can all be handled the same way. They long to be loved and valued as they are.

We must live in the tension between respecting the unique design that our artistic Creator crafted into the DNA of our children and building a bridge of love to their hearts so they will be more willing to listen to the messages we live and speak.

His Promises

The body has many different parts, not just one part. If the foot says, "I am not a part of the body because I am not a hand," that does not make it any less a part of the body. And if the ear says, "I am not part of the body because I am not an eye," would that make it any less a part of the body? If the whole body were an eye, how would you hear? Or if your whole body were an ear, how would you smell anything? But our bodies have many parts, and God has put each part just where he wants it.

1 CORINTHIANS 12:14-18

*Thank you for making me so wonderfully complex!
   Your workmanship is marvelous—how well I know it.*

PSALM 139:14

For there is one body and one Spirit, just as you have been called to one glorious hope for the future.

EPHESIANS 4:4

WINDOW
SEAT

There is a brief window of time when children are dependent upon their parents, believing everything they say and wanting to please them. This season goes by quickly, so we must prepare for the years when they will naturally begin to seek independence.

All teens, for example, must test what they have been taught and own what they really believe. Maneuvering through this transition with wisdom and faith is essential to coming out the other end with your relationship still intact.

It is important to talk to your children about all kinds of subjects before they hit those teenage years and to develop a trusting relationship with them where they can confide their fears, thoughts, negative feelings, and even doubts about God. If they know that you will not react in fear or lay guilt on them, they will know that you are their ally and will probably still want to talk to you about the mysterious issues of teenage life.

If they think you will get mad, make fun of them, yell, or not understand, often they will seek the input of others, who may or may not share your values.

Even though they may seem to be pushing you away, teens need you to walk beside them every step, to be involved in their lives, and to protect them from unnecessary scars. They need your advice and guidance to help them make wise decisions.

His Promises

Tune your ears to wisdom,
    and concentrate on understanding.

PROVERBS 2:2

Speak the truth in love, growing in every way more and more like Christ, who is the head of his body, the church.

EPHESIANS 4:15

So encourage each other and build each other up, just as you are already doing.

1 THESSALONIANS 5:11

CHOOSE
WISELY

It is essential that we fill our minds with biblical wisdom and not just man's advice. If you want to make wise decisions, you must adhere to the wisdom and insight of Scripture. Wisdom is at the core of living a righteous life and seeing God's favor unfold.

Don't be caught in confusion, looking for favor when you have lived unwisely. Choices have consequences. Seeking to become wise and humble, obediently listening to and following godly advice, is the only way to find a centered life with a foundation that will not be shaken.

Choosing love and service by modeling our lives after Christ is choosing to live wisely. We cannot compromise the truths and wisdom of God and expect to have the same consequences as if we had followed Him.

God is very patient and gracious, and He will restore and heal us over time. However, God is not Santa Claus, handing out answers to all requests just because we want something or have made a mess of something. He has made us in His image and given us the Spirit, so we are empowered to choose obedience, seek excellence of character, work hard, and keep our eyes on Him.

We are called to be stewards of the truth and wisdom He has provided. We must embrace responsibility for our lives. Our responsibility is to listen to His voice and follow His ways if we want to grow in order, strength, beauty, and soundness.

His Promises

But the wisdom from above is first of all pure. It is also peace loving, gentle at all times, and willing to yield to others. It is full of mercy and the fruit of good deeds. It shows no favoritism and is always sincere.

JAMES 3:17

Joyful is the person who finds wisdom,
*   the one who gains understanding.*
For wisdom is more profitable than silver,
*   and her wages are better than gold.*
Wisdom is more precious than rubies;
*   nothing you desire can compare with her.*
She offers you long life in her right hand,
*   and riches and honor in her left.*
She will guide you down delightful paths;
*   all her ways are satisfying.*
Wisdom is a tree of life to those who embrace her;
*   happy are those who hold her tightly.*

PROVERBS 3:13-18

Let the message about Christ, in all its richness, fill your lives. Teach and counsel each other with all the wisdom he gives. Sing psalms and hymns and spiritual songs to God with thankful hearts.

COLOSSIANS 3:16

SHOW ME
THE LOVE

Motherhood is such a demanding call, and we have so many tasks to complete. But all of our work will be in vain if we do not seek to show the children in our home the reality of God's joy, love, creativity, and life.

Our view of God is reflected in how we live life in front of our children each day.

God is the author of all creation, including waterfalls, roses, puppy dogs, lightning storms, color, sound, food, and all delights. He designed and gave us the instinct to giggle and belly laugh; to sway and swirl with the sounds of vibrant music; to delight in the galaxies aglow on a summer's night; to touch, kiss, hug, and love; to work and bring color, beauty, and skill into the presentation of a garden; to write a story; to set a beautiful table; to cook a meal that delights the palate; to nurse the ill back to health; and so much more. Our lives should reflect this greatness of God, this joie de vivre, through the ways we face and celebrate life each day.

Instead of gluing our faces to a screen, instead of focusing on the drudgery of the everyday, let's look deeply into the eyes of these creatures of God living in our home, see inside their hearts, and affirm the beauty we find there.

His Promises

Ask, using my name, and you will receive, and you will have abundant joy.

JOHN 16:24

I have told you these things so that you will be filled with my joy. Yes, your joy will overflow!

JOHN 15:11

You love him even though you have never seen him. Though you do not see him now, you trust him; and you rejoice with a glorious, inexpressible joy. The reward for trusting him will be the salvation of your souls.

1 PETER 1:8-9

TABLE OF CONTENTEDNESS

Our culture praises material possessions as a source of happiness. Those who have more are supposedly happier, and those who have less are somehow unjustly struggling. We believe a new house, a better car, or a larger salary will bring us happiness. Often, the longing for more things and money leads us to idolize wealth, work long hours to the detriment of our families, and seek a way to provide for ourselves instead of trusting God with our humble circumstances.

It is not sinful or wrong to have desires for something more in various areas of life. Our hearts can actually perceive a better world and more wonderful circumstances than we presently have because we were made for a better place. We were made for perfection, love, joy, and great blessing. It was in the heart of God to provide us a magnificent life.

The only way we will ever be able to be content, though, is to realize the nature of a fallen world.

This earth is not heaven. We must cultivate a level of thanksgiving and contentment in the life we have been given now. God calls us to find our contentment in Him, not in our circumstances or our material possessions. To choose to look beyond material possessions, to seek His fingerprints every day in our lives, to have an eternal perspective—this is the only way we will be able to be content.

His Promises

For the love of money is the root of all kinds of evil. And some people, craving money, have wandered from the true faith and pierced themselves with many sorrows.

1 TIMOTHY 6:10

Better to have little, with fear for the LORD,
*   than to have great treasure and inner turmoil.*

PROVERBS 15:16

Yet true godliness with contentment is itself great wealth. After all, we brought nothing with us when we came into the world, and we can't take anything with us when we leave it. So if we have enough food and clothing, let us be content.

1 TIMOTHY 6:6-8

WATCH THEM GROW!

When looking at a tiny seed, it is impossible to see what will grow from such a minute speck of nothing— the color of its blooms, the type of fruit, the size of the plant. There is vast potential locked within, and under the right circumstances—if it is planted in good soil, is watered regularly, and gets plenty of sunshine—a miracle will happen. The seed transforms into something more than itself.

God calls us to sow broadly, generously, diligently into the lives of our children.

We are asked to believe in the potential we sow, the latent miracles inside small life-seeds.

Our task is to be faithful to sow, by faith, the seeds of promise given to us; His is to do the miracle, to take all the seeds of faithfulness, love, and service and grow them into such a bounty of beauty. One day we will finally see that He was creating the miracle in our children; the seeds will sprout into a harvest of righteousness and redemption that will be beyond what we could have imagined.

So, dear God, let us look at the flowers You have planted and see beyond them to the beautiful harvest of our lives and the lives of our children, and help us believe in the potential of the seeds we are planting right now, which by faith will become a harvest of righteousness beyond measure.

His Promises

I pray that your love will overflow more and more, and that you will keep on growing in knowledge and understanding.

PHILIPPIANS 1:9

Now all glory to God, who is able, through his mighty power at work within us, to accomplish infinitely more than we might ask or think.

EPHESIANS 3:20

For we are God's masterpiece. He has created us anew in Christ Jesus, so we can do the good things he planned for us long ago.

EPHESIANS 2:10

About the Author

Sally Clarkson is the beloved author of multiple bestselling books, including *Girls' Club* with her daughters, Sarah and Joy; *The Lifegiving Home* with her daughter Sarah; *Desperate* with Sarah Mae; *Different* with her son Nathan; and *Own Your Life*. As a mother of four, she has inspired thousands of women through conferences, resources, and books with Whole Heart Ministries (www.wholeheart.org). She has also advocated relentlessly for the power of motherhood and the influence of home through her Mom Heart conferences (www.momheart.org), speaking to audiences on several continents.

Discipleship and mentoring women to understand how to love God in a more personal way and how to live a satisfying Christian life are threads through all of her messages. Sally encourages many through her blogs, podcasts, and websites. You can find her on her blog at www.sallyclarkson.com. Her popular podcast,

At Home with Sally Clarkson and Friends, which has over a million downloads, can be found on iTunes and Stitcher. She regularly teaches at conferences and on webcasts, and she participates in international discipleship ministry in venues all over the world.

Books by Sally Clarkson

OWN YOUR LIFE

THE LIFEGIVING HOME (with Sarah Clarkson)

THE LIFEGIVING HOME EXPERIENCE (with Joel Clarkson)

THE LIFEGIVING TABLE

THE LIFEGIVING TABLE EXPERIENCE (with Joel & Joy Clarkson)

THE LIFEGIVING PARENT (with Clay Clarkson)

THE LIFEGIVING PARENT EXPERIENCE (with Clay Clarkson)

DIFFERENT (with Nathan Clarkson)

A DIFFERENT KIND OF HERO (with Joel Clarkson)

THE MISSION OF MOTHERHOOD

THE MINISTRY OF MOTHERHOOD

YOU ARE LOVED BIBLE STUDY (with Angela Perritt)

DESPERATE (with Sarah Mae)

GIRLS' CLUB (with Joy & Sarah Clarkson)

GIRLS' CLUB EXPERIENCE (with Joy Clarkson)

MOM HEART MOMENTS

Visit her online at SALLYCLARKSON.COM.